101 Reasons Why You Should Not Become A Cop

101 Reasons Why You Should Not Become A Cop

James Richard Warner

iUniverse, Inc.
New York Lincoln Shanghai

101 Reasons Why You Should Not Become A Cop

iUniverse books may be ordered through booksellers or by contacting:

iUniverse
2021 Pine Lake Road, Suite 100
Lincoln, NE 68512
www.iuniverse.com
1-800-Authors (1-800-288-4677)

ISBN-13: 978-0-595-35136-7 (pbk)
ISBN-13: 978-0-595-79838-4 (ebk)
ISBN-10: 0-595-35136-0 (pbk)
ISBN-10: 0-595-79838-1 (ebk)

Printed in the United States of America

Contents

Acknowledgments

I would like to thank all the officers who shared their personal experiences. These officers told stories across the country and have made this work comprehensive, adding depth to understanding the contemporary problems of police work and the challenges that law enforcement presents to the new recruit.

Special thanks goes to David Kole, who inspired and supported all aspects of the work.

Introduction

So, you want to be a cop. Well, before you submerge yourself in this profession, let me, a nineteen-year veteran with several years of supervisory experience, give the prospective candidate some insight—insight that you will never hear from the recruiter, Golden Boy[1], or out-of-touch, pencil-pushing administrators. I want to make it clear that I'm not a disgruntled civil servant nor have I lamented the decision I made over nineteen years ago when I entered this profession. But over the past several years, when individuals have approached me and expressed an interest in becoming a police officer, I have been surprised to realize how much television and movies have shaped peoples' ideas of what a police officer experiences throughout his career.

The motivation to write this book was to inform the wannabe of the negatives they will encounter in a law enforcement career. That's right, I said *will encounter*—not *may encounter*. I have found in my experience that an officer will be subjected to 75 percent of the 101 reasons listed in this book and will know other cops or have partners who have suffered the aftereffects of the other 25 percent. These "reasons" are not necessarily arranged in any particular order. I have tried to list them in the order that a rookie police officer may encounter them—starting with the first reason, the Heavy Badge Syndrome, and continuing to

---

1.   *A Golden Boy is an individual who has been picked continually for choice assignments over more experienced cops and/or given the newest or best equipment. The Golden Boy is chosen, not based on his acumen or knowledge, but solely on who he knows. He could be a very good cop or a very inept one, but the one common denominator is that he is always chosen based on who, and not what, he knows. In addition, a Golden Boy will rarely receive discipline—or, if given discipline, it is only a fraction of what the average cop would receive. This occurs on the basis of favoritism.*

the fifty-second one, which illustrates how an officer takes an introspective inventory of his career after a number of years on the job. The last forty-nine reasons focus on situations that a police officer will confront after serving for many years. The "kicker" for officers is that these 101 reasons are not just one-time events, but most of the situations occur throughout an officer's career, illustrating the difficulty of being a police officer.

One of the interesting aspects of the *101 Reasons Why You Should Not Become a Police Officer* is the reasons are based on true experiences that officers across the country have faced. Whether an officer works in a small or large department, the negatives of a law enforcement career are encountered in similar situations. This book will elicit a wide range of reactions. For example, the veteran officer will find humor in many of the reasons, but the prospective police candidate will read many of the same reasons and be perplexed. Many police candidates have developed a stereotype of police work, constructed by years of watching police movies and reality shows that fail to unveil the truly negative aspects of a career in law enforcement. Consequently, whether you are reading for pleasure, a sense of support, or for information in determining whether a career in law enforcement is for you, I am sure everyone will walk away with a renewed perspective of the contemporary police officer.

The reasons listed do not necessarily stand alone; it is the totality of all the reasons that candidates should consider before making a decision to pursue a career in law enforcement. The candidate should expect to encounter situations similar to those listed and determine if he or she is willing to endure them by choosing this kind of career. I have written most of the reasons in the following format: first, a reason (a catch phrase); then, a description of what the reason is and how it manifests itself in the law enforcement field. Next, a true police officer story that relates to the reason, and then, how the reason will affect officers throughout their careers.

The reader should note that there are similarities between some of the reasons listed. Nevertheless, the qualitative difference of each story chosen for a particular reason was to demonstrate a specific circumstance officers will face during their careers. For example, reason seventy-six Giving up your rights and reason eighty-four Freedom of speech both explain how police officers individual freedoms are limited. Many of the stories told could be used to demonstrate other reasons, but each anecdote was chosen based on the subtle allegory of a specific reason.

Individuals motivated to pursue a career in law enforcement can be put into three categories: the person who has always wanted to be a police officer; the individual looking for a challenging, unobstructed work environment that appears to offer diverse situations from day to day; and the person searching for the secure government job. These three categories include just about every individual in police work. But rest assured, no matter what the person's motivation, there is no escaping the 101 reasons that will affect his or her career and life as a police officer.

Here Are 101 Reasons Why You Should Not Become a Police Officer

Reason One: The Heavy Badge Syndrome. This syndrome touches all new officers, but its effects and duration vary dramatically from person to person, based on an officer's past experience, maturity, and level of self-confidence.

The Heavy Badge Syndrome is a mind-set that starts near the end of academic training or right after—at the time when an officer starts to understand the fundamental concepts of his job but doesn't have the discretionary abilities or practical experience to discern where his duty ends and where playing the role of a good citizen begins. The process usually goes something like this: Having gone through a four-or a six-month academy that includes hundreds of hours of class instruction and firearms qualification, in addition to all the accoutrements that the job requires, the new officer believes he is anointed for the task of correcting every wrong he witnesses, whether on or off duty. In short, he is over-identifying—living the stereotype of a cop.

The best story that demonstrates the Heavy Badge Syndrome comes from a police officer in a medium-sized department in the Midwest:

After I graduated the academy, I felt great, believing that I found my niche in life. I was a full-fledged police officer and believed that it was my duty to stop crime whenever and wherever I saw it. I had the Heavy Badge Syndrome. Once, while stopped at a red light with my wife and son in the back seat, I saw a Mustang convertible pull up along the right side of my car. I looked over at the three occupants of the Mustang. I observed that the rear passenger was sitting on top of the seat, smoking what I knew was a joint of marijuana. Without a moment's thought, I jumped out of my car and approached the occupants of the vehicle. I pulled out my badge and walked up to the driver of the Mustang and directed the driver to pull off to the side of the road. The driver accelerated, making an abrupt right turn that almost tossed the rear passenger, who was still seated on top of the rear seat, out of the vehicle. I ran back to my vehicle to pursue the Mustang. As I caught up to the Mustang at the next traffic light, the driver of the Mustang ran the red light and caused an accident that seriously injured one of the passengers of the Mustang. Looking back on the situation, this was a poor decision on my part for a number of obvious reasons—not the least of which was putting my family in danger. After an internal investigation was conducted regarding my actions, I was fortunate enough to keep my job. But the department had to pay thousands of dollars in damages, and I had to endure several years fending off lawsuits and depositions.

The officer that told this story was lucky that he didn't lose his job. Although his heart was in the right place, he suffered from Heavy Badge Syndrome. A number of officers will be fired during their initial year, when rookie officers are most susceptible to the syndrome. Many new police officers do not have the maturity or experience to differentiate between when they should act as good citizens (witnesses) and when they should act as police officers. Only with experience will officers realize when they are in positions to act in a law enforcement capacity safely and effectively.

Reason Two: The neighborhood dispute. In most neighborhoods, there is one neighbor who is a thorn in everyone's side. The neighborhood dispute can become a big problem for the police officer who lives there. Everyone in the neighborhood will—or does—know that a cop lives in the neighborhood, and if an officer thinks they don't know, he'd better believe that they will find out.

Here is a story about an experience an officer had with a neighborhood dispute that didn't turn out the way he or his neighbors would have liked: *One of the officer's neighbors, who lived to the rear of his house, was a constant problem (e.g., loud parties and heavy traffic during all hours of the night). All the other neighbors constantly went to him to resolve the situation because he was a cop. He felt he was in the middle of the problem—confronted on the one side by the disruptive neighbor that he didn't like and on the other side by the rest of his neighbors. The disruptive neighbor just didn't fit into their neighborhood. The neighbors banded together and attempted to ostracize their nonconforming neighbor. Consequently, the disruptive neighbor began to retaliate, and he did anything and everything he could to cause problems. Herein lies the problem for the friendly neighborhood police officer. The disruptive neighbor discovered that one of the other neighbors heard he had a criminal record, and the rumors started to fly. The disruptive neighbor figured that the only one who could have known anything about his criminal history would be the cop who lived to the rear of his home. So the disruptive neighbor made a call to the officer's internal affairs complaint department, and the cop found himself in the position of defending himself and his reputation.*

The officer is in a no-win situation. On the one side, the disruptive neighbor will consider the officer's actions corrupt and think he is using his authority inappropriately and violating the public's trust. On the other side, if the officer fails to use his position and resources to correct the perceived disruptive neighbor behavior, the other neighbors will view him as ineffective. Whether the officer uses his resources or not, he will most likely become involved in an internal investigation that will question his actions or failure to act. If an officer runs a criminal record check on an individual for a non-related criminal matter, he is in violation of federal law and department policy. Officers are not allowed to run criminal history records except in a law enforcement capacity. Therefore, the neighbor dispute is always a situation for an officer to approach with caution.

Reason Three: Strippers, internal investigations, prison, and the untimely demise. At first, most potential police candidates may think there is no relationship between these words, but be assured, the seasoned officer knows the close tie these words have for the immature or womanizing officer.

The following story exemplifies this principle:

The officer—I will call him Mike—was smart and truly enjoyed his new career as a police officer. Other than the usual rookie mistakes, he tended to have good decision-making abilities in the field. This officer started to hang out around his beat strip clubs, just to have a few drinks with his squad after the shift. And as many young officers do, he became involved with one of the "stripper cop groupies." Strippers tend to be drawn to cops for a number of reasons, ranging from protection to a perception of power. The officer and the stripper he befriended—who I will call Sue—started dating on a regular basis. After several weeks, Sue started asking Mike for favors, such as loaning her money to pay the rent or borrowing his car to get to work. Mike began to fall hard for Sue. He always said, "She really knows how to treat a man." The other officers would say, "Yeah, I know, she's a stripper, that's what she gets paid to do—conning and manipulating you out of money, Mike!" Mike wouldn't even reply to the negative comments. After a couple of months, Mike found out Sue was hanging out with other guys at the club. Mike started getting jealous and spending more and more of his nights off at the club. Sue would continually reassure Mike that he was the only one for her, but that she had to pay attention to other men while she was working to make money for both of them. Mike began to understand her business and started to point out guys that he thought had money for Sue to "work." And thus began the downward spiral of Mike's demise, as Mike became part of the business. Mike began to understand that the nature of the business is to get what you can while you can; before Mike knew it, he would be "the mark[1]." Between both of them, they made enough money to buy expensive gifts, vacations, and cars. But then Sue started distancing herself from Mike. He became obsessive and started following her to and from work—even to the point of calling in sick just to check up on her. Sue knew exactly how she could get Mike off her back: by filing a complaint with the department and explaining how Mike would call in sick to hang out at the club and help her pick up men who had money to spend.

A few weeks later, Sue found another guy. Intoxicated, Mike went to Sue's apartment and initiated contact with her outside. He grabbed Sue and pulled her inside his vehicle, saying, "I just want to talk to you." In police work, we call this kidnapping, and so did the officers that responded to the call—the call that was initiated by the twenty witnesses outside the apartment complex.

Mike was taken into custody two days later, and Sue stated she did not want to press charges but just wanted Mike to leave her alone. However, Mike was prosecuted under a domestic violence statute and was found guilty.

---

1.   *"The mark" is a person who is targeted for a con.*

Although this story may appear to be an extreme example, there will always be officers that fall into the trap. The exceptions are rare, and every police officer will be able to talk about an officer who lost his career because he got involved with a stripper. The rule of thumb is that a cop is risking his career if he pursues such relationships.

Reason Four: "Hey, can you do me a favor?" These favors are requests that most people realize are not appropriate, but family and friends will ask officers for them time and again. For example, "Hey, can you run this guy for me?" "Hey, can you run this vehicle for me?" "Hey, can you find out why my brother, sister, or brother's sister's boy-friend is on probation?" Or, "Hey, can you find out if my daughter's friend has a criminal record?"

This story is told by a personal friend and officer:

The officer's brother's ex-wife's new boyfriend has entered the picture. The officer's brother wanted to know if the ex-wife's new boyfriend had any criminal history, because the boyfriend had contact with his daughters. The brother asked if he could run the boyfriend's vehicle plate and then run the person for any criminal record. The officer explained to the brother that checking a person's criminal history is against the law and he could get fired for violating a person's rights. The brother then stated that if he cared about him he would do it, and if he didn't do him the favor, he would find another cop to do it.

Being a police officer requires standing your ground and doing the right thing even though most of the time it will not be the most popu-lar thing to do when it involves family, friends, and neighbors. Police officers are strictly forbidden as stated previously, to use their position to access criminal history records on individuals for purposes other than police matters.

Reason Five: The other cop in the neighborhood: "What an assh-ole!" The odds are that if one police officer lives in the neighborhood, there will be another one living nearby. Most of the time this situation doesn't present any problems, but if one officer in the neighborhood decides he will become the off-duty parking enforcement officer and provide parking citations to your neighbors, this will cause several prob-lems. Police officers come with many different personalities. Some officers cannot separate their personal lives from their professional lives. The officer in the neighborhood who wants to conduct enforcement activities will cause the neighbors to go to the other officer, wanting to know what can be done to get the former officer off their backs.

The story that illustrates this situation goes like this:

Two officers, having worked together for several months, just realized they live three blocks away from each other. Having discovered the close proximity of his colleague, one officer invited the other over for coffee. Two days later, his neighbor approached him and asked why the officer living three blocks away wrote him a citation for his truck that was parked in front of his house. The officer told his neighbor that he didn't know the other officer wrote him a citation and that he would speak to the other officer. After the officer confronted his colleague, the officer that wrote the citationt stated that the neighbor's truck was illegally parked. The officer told his colleague that he didn't care how his neighbor parked. His colleague replied that the neighbor was parked illegally and the law must be enforced, and said he would start to check all the vehicles in the neighborhood for vio-lations. The officer replied, "That's great, but stay off my street."

As stated previously, police officers have different personality types. Most of the time having a fellow officer living nearby doesn't present a problem, but if an officer sees himself as working twenty-four hours a day, seven days a week, enforcing any and every violation that he witnesses, it can present a difficult situation—one in which the neighbors will look to the other officer for relief.

Reason Six: The "once a cop" story: "Once a cop stopped me for no reason, took me to jail for no reason, hit me for no reason," etc. The story is something officers better get used to from the get-go. Officers call this reason "the story," and everyone will have some story of how they were stopped and harassed by "the man" for absolutely "no reason at all." After some time on the job officers will learn that these stories usually don't hold water.

An incident that demonstrates the story goes something like this:

I was out with a couple of friends at the local coffee house, enjoying a day off and a nice cup of fresh-brewed, house blend coffee, when we ran into a friend of a friend who decided to join us. After learning I was the cop in the group, "the friend" decided to vent his frustration with the local authorities on me. He started his story of how he was driving downtown, and of course, obeying all the local laws and ordinances, when a motorcycle cop pulled him over. He continued, "This cop jumped off his motorcycle, ran up to me and started to scream at me for no reason, no reason at all. He then towed my car and left me on the side of the road." After the storyteller finished, I decided to ask a few questions—not hard ones, just some basic questions. For example, what was the cop screaming, and did you make a complaint on the officer? Did he give you a citation or a copy of the tow report? Well, this was a lesson hard learned for me, because the person telling the story doesn't care about anything a cop has to say, much less anyone questioning his veracity. He only wants you to agree that all cops are assholes.

The moral for any person wanting to enter law enforcement is to realize that the individual is telling a story of how he thinks he was treated unfairly by cops. The officer who engages the storyteller in an argument is wasting his time, because the storyteller will never accept that anything he did was wrong. The best defense is just to agree and nod your head.

Reason Seven: "I know you're eating, and you look really busy writing those reports, but can I ask you a question?" Redundant questions are just one of the many things that come with the job, because unlike most other professionals, a cop in uniform is a magnet for questions. Maybe the gun hanging off his waist gives it away, along with the badge and all that neat stuff attached to the officer's belt. Just know that everywhere an officer goes, somebody wants to approach an officer and ask a question, a question the officer has answered a million and one times.

The story that every officer will experience goes like the following scenario, told by a patrol officer about one time when he was eating lunch with his partner:

All it took was for one of us to make eye contact with a guy sitting across the restaurant. After I made eye contact with the guy I knew he would take the opportunity to engage us with the "question." I said under my breath to my lunch mate, "You take this one, because here he comes." And, yes, you guessed right, the question asked was "Hey, what kind of gun do you carry?" The officer thinks, "If only I had one share of Microsoft for every gun question asked." The officer forces a smile and acts like he has never been asked that one before, as the guy stands at the table for about half the meal before he gets the hint that the food is cold.

A uniformed police officer will come to realize that there is no anonymity. Wherever the officer goes and whatever he does, he is in view of the public. There are many days that an officer might just want to blend in, but as long as the officer is working in a patrol vehicle and wearing a uniform, there is no escaping the eyes of the public or the guy who wants to ask the questions that officers must answer over and over again.

Reason Eight: Bite your lip. Most police officers have had to deal with a citizen who thinks he knows more about law and law enforcement than the officer knows. In these situations the officer must contest with two issues: first, more than likely the officer will be on a call and have to control other individuals, and second, the officer must deal with the know-it-all who has way too much time on his hands and has seen every rerun of every cop show. Of course, after watching these television shows, the guy knows more about the law and police work than he thinks the officer will ever be able to comprehend.

The situation that best describes the "bite your lip" scenario was told by a colleague of mine who was attempting to resolve a rental dispute:

The owner of the rental property wanted the renter out—evicted from his rental house. And the owner of the property had been to court on several occasions to begin eviction proceedings, but he never completed or obtained the court order or documentation necessary to complete the eviction. The officer met the owner at a nearby Stop & Shop. The owner demanded the officer to follow him to his rental to throw the renters out. In addition, the owner began to tell the officer that, if he didn't comply, the owner would sue the officer for any damage to his house that was caused by the renter. The officer patiently explained to the owner that he must obtain the correct documentation to evict the renter. The owner would not listen to the officer's attempts to explain the process, and continued to cite laws that he believed should be enforced by the officer. The owner, becoming more and more frustrated with the officer, contacted his attorney while talking to the officer, and then demanded that the officer speak to his attorney on his cell phone. After the officer spoke to the owner's attorney, the officer told the owner that his attorney agreed with the officer. The owner continued to argue and threatened to sue the officer for failing to follow his interpretation of the law.

The "bite your lip" scenario is a lose-lose situation for police officers. If the officer continues to argue with a citizen, he will surely find himself with an internal investigation being filed against him for losing his temper. Second, the officer will never be able to reason with an individual who is arguing from an emotional point of view. Therefore, the best course of action for an officer in this lose-lose situation is to walk away and "bite his lip" after explaining the facts to the individuals involved.

Reason Nine: No one wants you around in the good neighborhood. The fact is that although most people who live in "good neighborhoods" support the police, vote yes on pro-police issues, and are the first to approach officers and thank them for doing a great job, but they don't want the cops in their neighborhoods. Why? Because the police are a sign that something is wrong, that something has happened. The police must be there because something bad has occurred, and that means "there goes the neighborhood." People in those neighborhoods see a marked patrol unit as evidence that their home may be losing value by the hour, and/or the area is being to change for the worst.

A story illustrating this situation was told by an officer passing through a middle class community, just killing some time before securing (end of shift) after a graveyard shift:

The officer noticed a resident staring at him like he had never seen a police car—no wave, no head nod, just a stare as his eyes tracked the officer's every move across the front curtilage. As the officer continued his slow patrol, he noticed another resident waving his hands in an attempt to get the officer's attention. The officer slowly pulled up to the edge of the sidewalk, barely coming to a stop before the resident asked the officer, "What happened, what's going on?" And the officer replied, "Nothing, nothing at all, just patrolling the neighborhood." The resident replied apprehensively, "Oh, I just don't see you guys around here."

The reality is that police officers working in a large metropolitan area don't have the time to patrol the "good neighborhoods"; therefore, local residents will not be accustomed to seeing police in those areas. In addition, when people see a police car, it usually means trouble is not far away.

Reason Ten: No one wants you around in the bad neighborhood. Police officers realize poorer communities have trepidation when there are police activities in their neighborhood. It's the kind of apprehensiveness experienced when a driver notices a police car in their rearview mirror. A driver may not be doing anything wrong, but there's still a natural nervousness when a police car is behind his or her car.

The best story I've heard regarding this reason is of a day-shift officer patrolling early one morning in an inner city neighborhood, and it was told as follows:

The officer began driving slowly by a local school bus stop, observing the children and parents patiently awaiting the school bus. The officer noticed that very few if any of the children waved and the parents purposely avoided eye contact. The officer passed the bus stop and glanced in his rearview mirror. The officer just had to laugh at the children's response to his passing, never forgetting the difficulty the children had, extending their arms upward, arduously attempting to maintain their middle fingers extending upward (Flipping the Bird). The hubristic parents acted as though their children had just been received into an Ivy League school.

Police realize that their presence is not always welcome in certain areas. But no matter how some communities respond to the police, a police officer must always provide the highest quality service possible. Poorer communities react to police based on stereotypes and propaganda. If an officer believes that he can change a community's beliefs, he will surely become frustrated and disappointed.

Reason Eleven: The cop, the hypocrite. Police officers can easily fall into a trap that will result in hypocritical actions. Police officers must continually reevaluate their actions to avoid the appearance of bias.

For example, officers usually don't think twice about accepting free meals on duty, getting free drinks, coffee, and so on. Some officers, while on duty, will only patronize businesses that dole out free services. Consequently, many of these officers will not patronize businesses that do not offer such services. Officers who only patronize businesses that provide complementary services and avoid businesses that don't provide free services are being hypocrites. Officers who only frequent businesses that provide complementary services have compromised their ethics to be fair, firm, and consistent with all members within the community they serve. The altered behavior is caused by bias, or at least others perceive it to be. Businesses that do not provide perks observe officers patronizing businesses that do provide complementary services and therefore view the officers' behavior as corrupt.

The following story demonstrates the hypocritical officer:

An officer conducting traffic enforcement performed a traffic stop. The driver of the stopped vehicle was a manager of a local coffee shop that provided free coffee to officers. The officer was known as a "hard ass," meaning that he never gave anybody he stopped a warning. The officer had the motto: "If I stop 'em, I ticket 'em." But the officer gave a warning to this driver.

Whether the officer in this scenario gave the driver a warning based on his employment or based on the officer's discretionary power is a moot point. The problem lies in the appearance of the officer's actions being hypocritical. Police officers must always be self-aware and evaluate their actions when performing enforcement duties, and ensure their behavior is consistent and fair with all citizens. Even the perception of bias can reflect on an officer's and a police department's integrity.

Reason Twelve: "I'll have your job." Officers can count on hearing this one time and time again. The "I'll have your job" threat is common in many professional settings, but police officers hear it constantly throughout their careers. Citizens that use the threat are attempting to intimidate the officer into doing or not doing his duty. A citizen will also use the threat in an attempt to get the officer's "goat," hoping that he will react in an unprofessional manner, so the citizen has the ammunition to file a complaint against the officer. The threat is used by all types of individuals—rich or poor, stone-cold sober or drunk.

Traffic officers or motorcycle units hear the threat "I'll have your job" the most. The officer who told this story worked as a motorcycle cop for four years. The following incident occurred when the officer was working a high-accident area, attempting to write quality citations—not cheap, easy citations such as cracked-windshield or broken-taillight infraction violations. As the story goes:

When working radar he saw a black BMW traveling 55 mph in a 35 mph zone. After stopping the vehicle, he approached it, automatically giving his standard "spill" to the driver: "Sir, I stopped you for traveling 55 in a 35 mph zone. I need to see your..." and so on. The driver was rather courteous and polite, so the officer wrote the citation for only ten miles an hour over the speed limit rather than twenty. Returning to the driver, the officer began explaining the citation process, when the driver exploded with a symphony of profanities that would have made a sailor proud. The officer was stunned and could not believe this was the same guy he had just contacted. Then it came out. Right after the officer said, "Sir, you still need to sign the citation," the driver replied, "I'll have your job." The officer replied, "You're the second person today to have my job—have a good day."

Police officers will never escape the threats, and citizens will continue to use them in an attempt to intimidate officers. Officers must just learn to live and work with threats and hope whoever makes the threats doesn't have any leverage with the police department to carry them out.

Reason Thirteen: "I know the sheriff, chief, etc...." This threat is not as popular as the previous one, but officers will no doubt hear it from time to time. Of course, the purpose of a citizen saying that they know the head honcho is to intimidate officers into doing or not doing something.

A common situation in which an officer will hear this threat—told by an officer I met years ago, who is now retired told this story:

After the officer responded to a domestic call, he began to conduct an interview with the male involved in the domestic situation, noting that the subject was extremely intoxicated and could be described as…well, let's just say an ass! Although a battery didn't occur between the two parties involved, the officer knew that if he left the residence he would be called back to the home because the male wanted to continue to argue with his wife. Therefore, the officer made a decision to arrest the male for his outstanding traffic warrants. As the male was being handcuffed, he exclaimed, "I know the police chief and he will hear about this. The officer replied, "Oh yeah? Well, I will tell him 'hi' for you when I see him and his wife for dinner tonight." What the guy didn't know was that the officer making the arrest was the chief's brother-in-law.

Although the officer was in fact the brother-in-law of the police chief, most of the time officers will not have such a relationship and perhaps will never even have an opportunity to meet the police chief. Police officers must understand that some individuals will say or do just about anything to intimidate the police. Officers must understand that a large majority of the threats are hollow, but there will be times that the threats are not idle.

Reason Fourteen: The guy who really does know the sheriff, chief, etc…This is one of those reasons that can have a dramatic effect on a police officer's career. This reason demonstrates that no matter where an officer works, if he handles a situation wrong or right, it could set the tone for the rest of the officer's career.

This story comes from a cop who had been working for a small department in the northeast:

The officer was working a graveyard shift and noticed a J.D.L.R. (Just Doesn't Look Right)[2] vehicle. After the officer established probable cause he conducted a vehicle stop. The officer contacted the driver and began to question him to find out if he was on the up-and-up asking the routine questions: Where are you coming from, where are you going, do you own this car, and so on. The officer became suspicious of the driver because he wasn't quick enough in his responses, so the officer continued the questioning and requested that the driver return to the front of his patrol vehicle for further investigation. As the officer was escorting the driver to the front of the patrol vehicle, the driver stated that he knew the sheriff. The officer said, "What? I'm supposed to be impressed?" After thirty minutes of questioning, the driver was issued a citation for a minor infraction and released.

When the officer secured for the night, his sergeant called him into the office and inquired about the vehicle stop made earlier in the shift. The officer replied, "Yeah, no big deal—I followed this guy until I was able to establish probable cause and made contact with the driver, who told me he 'knew the sheriff.'" The sergeant quickly replied, "He does know the sheriff, and the captain called me, wanting to know what the situation was." The officer explained that he wasn't rude or anything, but was only trying to get some good stops and develop something.

Police work is fraught with this type of situation, because an officer never knows who he is dealing with and the officer's actions can and

---

2.   *The J.D.L.R. or suspicious vehicle is the bread and butter of police work. It can be described as an older model car with two or three different colored panels, signs of a recent collision that indicate a possible hit-and-run, and/or a driver who is attempting to act as if he doesn't notice a police officer, even when the officer has pulled up next to the driver at a traffic light.*

will be exaggerated by the average citizen. If an individual has contacts within the police administration, an officer can count on that person to make a phone call to whomever they know and complain about the officer's actions. The problem that occurs for an officer in such situations is that he may never know what that person may have said to "the boss." The officer in the above story has not been able to transfer or move to any specialized unit for over three years and believes it all stems from that one traffic stop. The officer never found out what the driver he'd stopped said about him to the sheriff, but he thinks something was said that has prevented him from advancement.

Reason Fifteen: "You cops are killing my business—but thank God you're here!" Police candidates intuitively think this would not be a common event regarding police presences, but rest assured it is quite commonplace. Police often patronize convenience stores and the like for a variety of reasons—to get out of the cold, the heat, or just to take a break between calls. The average citizen may think store employees and shop owners would want to have a police officer present in their business and encourage officers to patronize their businesses. This sentiment is not always the case, and such cases can be disconcerting to new officers if they do not have the experience to notice the nonverbal signs that communicate that the officer's presence is not welcome.

The following story illustrating this reason comes from a very good friend of mine who has been a police officer for over nineteen years:

Two officers decided to take a break at one of the local convenience stores, just to grab a soda and stretch their legs. When driving up to the store, they noticed that there were several vehicles in the parking lot and a few customers walking around inside the store. After spending a few minutes in the store, the officers noticed that all the cars and customers had left. One officer attempted to make small talk with the clerk behind the counter, but the clerk was short with his responses and the officers thought that he was simply having "just one of those days." After a few minutes, one of the officers commented to the clerk that business appeared slow. The clerk responded abruptly, "You're killing my business!" The officers did not think they heard the clerk correctly and replied simultaneously, "What?" The clerk reiterated the statement, which inflamed one of the officers, and he was about to tell the clerk what he thought of him. Luckily the other officer stepped up quickly, patted his fellow officer on his shoulder, and said, "Okay, we will leave now."

After a couple of days, both officers were notified that the clerk made a complaint about the officers staying at his business for an extended period. An internal investigation was completed and found that the officers had both checked out over their radios during the time they entered the store and were only at the business for a few minutes. The investigation did not find them to be neglectful, considering the time of night and that no calls for service were outstanding in their areas.

The ironic twist to the story is that exactly one week after the incident with the clerk, the clerk was robbed in the convenience store. The two officers the clerk complained about were the first officers to respond to the robbery scene. The arriving officers observed the clerk physically shaking, his eyes larger than doughnuts, and barely able to speak to the officers. Of course, both officers were thinking, "I bet you're glad to see us now," but they resisted making the comment.

The moral of the story is for potential police candidates to realize that police presence is not always welcome in every business or that employees do not always want officers around. Officers must learn to understand this apparent hypocrisy by citizens, and if an officer chooses not to understand it, it will eat away at the officer for the rest of his career.

Reason Sixteen: The Cop's Wife Syndrome. This reason is labeled as a syndrome because it occurs and may reoccur only under a specific set of circumstances. Officers' supervisors usually deal with this reason (syndrome). Of course, this reason could have also been called "the Cop's Husband Syndrome," but the syndrome occurs more commonly with wives than husbands. The syndrome manifests itself in a couple of ways. The most common is when an on-duty police officer comes into contact with the wife of a cop in some situation like a traffic stop for speeding, running a red light, or any number of minor incidents. The officer that conducts the traffic stop maintains his professionalism as he would with any citizen, being fair, firm, and consistent. Most officers do not issue a citation to the wife of a fellow officer, for obvious reasons. But if during the traffic stop, the wife doesn't identify herself to the officer conducting the stop, she could receive a citation or other enforcement actions. A wife receiving a citation from a traffic stop can create several problems. One of these problems is that she must return home to face the husband and relay the news that she was administered a citation by another police officer. Usually the wife, knowing and expecting her husband to be extremely upset with the actions that led to her contact with the police officer, will attempt to obfuscate the incident with a diversion. The most common diversion is to lie about the cop who stopped her and describe him as unprofessional, rude, or "acting like an asshole" to her during the traffic stop. Therefore, the husband's anger shifts from his wife's driving behavior that led to the enforcement action to the officer that stopped his wife. This is the syndrome in a nutshell—it is an attempt to obfuscate a situation and shift the husband's anger from his wife to the cop who issued a citation to the wife.

This occurs quite frequently and such an incident resulted in the following story, told by a police supervisor:

One of my officers was working the graveyard shift during a rainy, cold, night, when he received an accident call described as a single vehicular accident and unknown injuries. After arriving on the call, the officer discovered that the vehicle was traveling too fast, which caused the driver to lose control of the vehicle, slide off the shoulder of the road, and collide with a small traffic sign. The accident caused moderate damage to the vehicle, and the driver needed a tow truck. The officer spoke to the female driver and asked if she was injured and in need of transportation after the tow truck responded. The officer completed the call and did not write her a citation for the accident, because there were no other vehicles involved and the damage to the vehicle was enough to teach a hard lesson.

Of course, the above story sounds harmless. Well, the next day I got a call from an officer who said his wife was involved in an accident and that one of my officers responded to the scene. He added that his wife told him that the officer was extremely rude and did not offer her additional assistance, and that his wife was pregnant. He added that the officer conducting the investigation of his wife's accident did not even offer to let her sit inside the patrol vehicle, making her stand outside in the cold, rainy weather instead. The officer making the complaint believed that the investigating officer may have been a rookie who failed to take appropriate actions.

I listened to the officer making the complaint and then posed a couple of questions of my own. After speaking with the aforementioned officer, I went to the officer who responded to the call. I told him that the female involved in the accident was the wife of a cop in the department and that she told her husband that he was rude and failed to offer her assistance out of the rain.

He responded by saying that he had no idea she was pregnant and he recalled asking her twice if she need anything. He stated that she always replied that she did not want anything. The officer asked me if her husband was going to file an official internal complaint and that he could not believe that she had told her husband that he had been rude. He adamantly expressed to me that he tried to be as helpful and professional as he could have been. I replied to him that the wife may have been just attempting to avoid the frustration of her husband after having been involved in an accident. The officer agreed that might be the situation, but her husband would always think that the officer had been rude to his wife. I replied that would probably be the case, but if he attempted to rectify the situation with the husband, he would be risking a potential official complaint. More than likely the husband would side with his wife. The officer agreed and decided to let the situation go.

Most officers will encounter the Cop's Wife Syndrome at least once in their career. The incidents usually leave both officers frustrated and bitter toward each other. Although officers are trained to hear both sides of a story, officers can bet that when an incident involves another cop's family member, the officer who initiated enforcement action would most likely be described as the biggest jerk on the force.

Reason Seventeen: The cop who knows it all—"Just leave me alone!" The cop who knows it all, or thinks he knows it all, is just one of those personalities that other cops will have to work with. A situation will occur when the know-it-all works closely with another officer, that is, on the same squad. The know-it-all usually becomes attached to another officer and will attempt to arrive on calls with that officer, even though the call doesn't require a backup. When he does arrive on the call with the officer, the officer finds that the know-it-all will second-guess his every decision.

A situation that describes this reason best was told to me some years ago by an officer who found himself working with a know-it-all:

An officer just transferred to a new station. The officer was becoming acclimated to the new station and patrol area by inquiring about the locations of the high crime areas. Another officer, the know-it-all on the squad, misconstrued his inquisitiveness as insecurity. The know-it-all continually arrived on the officer's calls, and after the call he would tell how he would have handled it and how the decision that the officer made was not as good has what he would have done. The situation became so unbearable that even on high priority calls, the officer would race to the call and cancel the know-it-all before he could arrive. But this tactic did not always work because he would arrive anyway. The guy just would not take a hint. Not even a very direct hint, such as "Hey, stay away from me" and "Leave me alone."

The know-it-all occurs in most professions and every employee deals with this type of individual differently. But police work and how an officer handles the know-it-all can affect the officer's safety decisions, thus putting the officer in a dangerous situation.

Reason Eighteen: Officer Macho: "Hey, Rookie"—when this guy has one more day on the job than you do. Here again we have a situation that is related to the various types of personality traits that officers will deal with throughout their career. Police work is generally viewed as a masculine profession, and officers will encounter this macho attitude throughout their career, so be prepared for it.

The story I will tell here is from an officer I have known for many years, as he experienced this:

The officer was assigned to a day-shift squad, where the average officers were on the squad about three years. There are areas and assignments that require officers to be assigned to ride with a fellow squad member. Usually in this situation everyone on the squad has someone that they have developed a working relationship with and those officers would work together for the shift. But the officer was on the squad a short time and hadn't developed a connection with any of the other officers on the squad. Usually, in such a situation, the one officer that no one else wants to work with will work with the newest officer on the squad. There are a number of reasons why other officers don't want to work with Officer Macho, like he's arrogant, obnoxious, or heavy-handed behaviors toward citizens.

After three weeks of riding together and having his partner, Officer Macho, consistently pointing out how great a cop he is during the entire shift, the final straw came. They responded to a domestic call. After separating the two parties for interviews and Officer Macho completed his interview, he barked out "Hey, Rookie, go get some voluntary reports." Well, of course, there is no way that an officer would let that comment go, and he replied with, "Rookie, huh? Weren't you in the same academy as me? Why don't YOU go and get the reports?"

After the officers cleared the call and left the residence, the officer, having endured three weeks of macho crap, had some choice words for his partner. The officer believed he had endured enough and told the supervisor that, "Unless you give me a direct order, I'm not going to work with that guy another day." The supervisor understood without any explanation, and for the rest of the time on that squad he worked alone.

The moral to this story is that these kinds of officers don't "get it" and never will. They will constantly attempt to prove what great cops they are. Police work is stressful because the majority of the time the officer must constantly handle irate, angry, and disturbed individuals. Also having to work with Officer Macho is enough to change the most positive person into a negative and bitter employee.

Reason Nineteen: The lies—get use to it. The fact is that many of the people police officers encounter will lie. They will lie about their name, their date of birth, where they live, where they're going, and where they came from. This consistent deception occurs because it is often the nature of the people police encounter. Officers will even come to learn that people who have nothing to hide have developed such a habit of lying to the police, that they will lie to officers even when they don't need to try to hide anything, and this can be extremely frustrating for new officer to get accustomed to.

The story I will tell here involves an incident told by a partner of mine, involving a situation in which a subject pointed a firearm at another person:

The officers arrived on the shooting call that involved two ex-friends who were arguing over property. The suspect was standing outside a residence, where he allegedly pulled a gun on the person reporting the crime. The suspect arrived at his ex-friend's residence because of a dispute over property that the suspect claimed was inside his ex-friend's residence. After the officers arrived, they separated the parties and began conducting interviews. At first, the officer who interviewed the suspect didn't believe a word he said, but after several minutes the officer started to buy the story the suspect told him, which was that he never had a firearm and only came over to the residence to talk to his friend about retrieving his property. However, the other officer who arrived on the scene made contact with the resident who told the officer that the suspect did have a firearm and pointed it at him, demand-

ing that he give up the property in dispute. Both of the officers came together after the initial interviews to discuss the situation and find out the real story. The officer who spoke to the suspect tried to convince the other officer that he believed the suspect, adding that no gun was found during a pat down. In addition, the suspect stated he never would have pointed a gun at anybody. The officer that interviewed the resident/victim told the other officer that he appeared to be telling the truth. But the other officer would not budge, believing the suspect. Thus, instead of arresting the suspect, the resident was given a report and the officers cleared the call.

After four hours the officer who had interviewed the suspect received a call from dispatch telling him to call a witness who was near the residence when the event occurred. The officer called the witness, a UPS driver who had seen the suspect walking away from the residence with a firearm in his hand. The officer then knew that he had been duped by the suspect, and buying into everything the suspect had said.

This story illustrates a typical situation that police officers must deal with on a daily basis. The rule of thumb that officers will learn is to believe no one and assume that everyone is lying until they can prove otherwise. New officers will have difficulty adjusting to this concept, because most individuals are not accustomed to people lying to them, much less lying to a police officer, and it's hard when they discover the majority of individuals they contact will lie to them. The officer who has a hard time adjusting to this deceptive environment will become depressed and have difficulty in separating his work from his personal life.

Reason Twenty: "Is everyone lying to me?" After a police officer starts his or her police career, sooner or later they will start to develop certain skills, which include interviewing and interrogation techniques that the officer will use to catch the criminal in lies. These techniques will become a part of the officer's personality and will, after time, become pervasive throughout the officer's professional and personal life. As mentioned in the previous reason, many of the individuals whom officers come in contact with will lie. Consequently, if the officer is not careful, he will begin to ask himself, "Is everyone lying to me?" This reason can manifest with everyone the officer comes in contact with—his wife, his girlfriend, his significant other, and his friends. The stories collected with regard to this particular reason were numerous, but the best story was chosen to give the prospective candidate insight into what a police officer will begin to feel after just a short period of time on the force.

The following story is from an officer's personal experience, as he began to develop behaviors that caused major problems in his personal relationships:

The officer had a fantastic relationship with his wife and children. The couple had what was described as excellent communication between them and they always seemed to be able to talk things out. After her husband had a year on the job, his wife noticed a change in the way he spoke with her in routine conversations, but because the change was so gradual she didn't make much of it. However, one evening she came home from work and was a little later than normal. Her husband, the officer, began to question the whys and wherefores of her tardiness. She then began to understand he was speaking to her as if she were a suspect, and noticed the connection because of the stories he told her over the past year about interviewing suspects. She quickly pointed out the fact that she will not be spoken to in such a fashion, and her husband began to laugh, as he just then realized that his wife was correct and he had unwittingly been questioning her as if she were a suspect.

Police work requires officers to develop techniques to question suspects and witnesses, to find out what the truth is and who is lying. The skills, once developed, do not turn on and off. Officers must realize that these skills will manifest themselves in their personal lives and will be construed by others as him treating his friends and family as if they were suspects. This behavior is very serious and can be a factor that leads to friends distancing themselves and straining many of a police officer's relationships.

Reason Twenty-One: The kiss-ass. As in any other business, the kiss-ass is always an omnipresent personality on the police force. The only difference is that when an officer is identified as a kiss-ass, it always appears to be more distasteful than when others do it. The fact is that this tactic of sucking up does pay off, because people are people and some supervisors will buy into the kiss-ass and forget about the effects that the kiss-ass has on the morale of the other officers.

The story that demonstrates this reason comes from a good friend and fellow officer, and this is how he told me the story about this particular kiss-ass:

The officer was working on a squad for several months and came to know his squad members' personalities, as an officer would, over time. The one officer of topic, the kiss-ass, would always sit in the briefing room, within the sergeant's view. When the lieutenant would attend a briefing, the kiss-ass would be sitting in the front row, right in front of the lieutenant. Whether during briefing or debriefing, if a supervisor was present, he would always have something to add to the conversation regarding how many arrests he had made or how he could hook up the supervisor with a "deal" at a local retailer. But one day at a debriefing, the squad sergeant had had enough and said to the kiss-ass, "You are such a kiss-ass!" The kiss-ass replied, "Yeah, I know, but I'm good at it!" The rest of the squad couldn't believe he admitted it, and the officer telling the story just thought to himself, "Now that's tragic."

Police officers encounter the same personality problems as any other profession. The kiss-ass is usually a problem in police work because he is spending the majority of his time sucking up to supervisors rather than doing his job. Unfortunately, many supervisors are susceptible to the kiss-ass tactic and bamboozled by the kiss-ass. Many police supervisors are not willing to confront the kiss-ass and just ignore their behavior. When a supervisor does not recognize the signs of a kiss-ass, he will usually overlook the lack of performance by this officer, and other officers will become disconnected from the supervisor's goals. As stated before, all professions have kiss-asses, but when the kiss-ass is a cop it seems to be more distasteful and affect the working environment more than in other professional settings.

Reason Twenty-Two: The nerdy cop. Although the nerd is prevalent in most professions, it is a personality type that has a unique characteristic within law enforcement. Specifically, the nerdy cop may be an individual who has been motivated to be a cop for reasons that are self-serving—to overcome years of being the guy who was always picked on in school or always the last guy to be picked for the basketball team. The nerdy cop is attempting to conceal his own personal feelings of inadequacy. He uses his position to overcompensate and retaliate for what he believes are the wrongs that have been done to him in the past. Officers will recognize this personality easily because it manifests in various situations—for example, arresting someone when a warning would

be appropriate or writing multiple citations when a warning or one citation would be proper protocol.

The following story is told by a California trooper:

This cop must have been beaten up every day in school, because he would make more arrests on misdemeanor traffic stops than anybody the Ca. Trooper had ever worked with. On one particular day, the trooper was riding with the nerdy cop as he conducted a traffic stop on a speeder. As the nerdy cop approached the driver's side window, the trooper approached the passenger side. The driver was described by the trooper as being a very large guy. And right from the start, the nerdy cop started in on the driver: "Where do you think you're going in such a hurry? You're driving reckless! Where did you get your license?" As the nerdy cop continued, the driver had enough and told the nerdy cop, "If you're going to write me a ticket, then do it—otherwise I don't want to hear it." This statement was interpreted as disrespectful by the nerd. The nerdy cop then began an inspection of his vehicle, resulting in the driver receiving several minor citations for nonmoving violations. The backup trooper told the nerdy cop after the stop that he was out of line and unprofessional, but, "It's your stop, and I hope you can sleep at night."

The unfortunate aspect of the nerdy cop is that he will almost never overcome or grow out of the "get back at you" mentality. He never gets the respect he yearns for from peers or citizens, mainly because he does not treat others with the same courteousness or professionalism that he expects. The nerdy cop will be warned throughout his career about treating people disrespectfully, and the decisions he makes on calls will be difficult for other officers to accept. The decisions made by the nerdy cop will almost always be to apply extreme penalties when lesser penalties would accomplish the mission of the department. The nerdy cop is just another personality type that will create much frustration for other officers while they attempt to apply the law as fairly and equitably as possible.

Reason Twenty-Three: The supervisor who can't make a decision. One might think the nature of police work would help police officers develop the fundamental ability to make decisions and make them rather quickly. But as many of the previous reasons have stated, police officers are not immune from common corporate traits that are problematic to management. Although managers or supervisors who can't make decisions are common in the private sector, many people don't expect a police supervisor to be indecisive—and when they are, the problem appears to be magnified and more problematic. Because the expectations of police supervisors are higher than those for the typical corporate manager, police supervisors, if viewed as indecisive, will quickly lose credibility in the eyes of their subordinates.

One of the best stories relating this reason goes like this:

An officer responded to a civil disturbance call involving a civilian court order, signed by a judge, who ordered the removal of property from a residence. The order stated that all peace officers will enforce the following order or be held in contempt of court. The officer was confused with the legalese written in the court order and what his role in the order should be, and so, he called his supervisor. The supervisor told the officer, "Do what you think is best." The officer stood by to keep the peace between the two parties involved, while one of the two parties involved removed the property listed in the court order. Then the officer cleared the call without further incident. Two months later the officer was called into the supervisor's office. The supervisor advised him that the court order should not have been enforced and one of the parties made a complaint stating that the order was rescinded. The officer reminded the supervisor that he asked his advice as to enforcing the order. The supervisor told the officer that he remembered the call and told the officer, "Well, I guess you shouldn't have enforced the court order."

At first you may conclude that the supervisor who can't make a decision has a problematic personality, but that is not always the case. One of the major causes of indecisiveness is the administration of the police department and how other supervisory personnel have been treated by the administration when faced with a supervisory decision. If the administration is seen as unforgiving and quick to discipline supervisory personnel for making a wrong decision, this environment will surely add to the frustration of the line officer. When officers attempt to get guidance from their supervisors, the supervisors will often just say, "Do what you think is right," and then the officer will be the one left holding the proverbial bag.

Reason Twenty-Four: "I'll sue you." This is another one of those gems that officers hear over and over again. But unfortunately, getting sued is part of the job. Most of the time when a police officer is sued, the police department is also named in the lawsuit. The majority of the time when officers are named in a lawsuit they have not violated department policy or any laws if viewed from a law enforcement standpoint. The lawyers that prey on police departments don't look at police officers' actions from a law enforcement viewpoint. They line up at the public trough, hoping to extort money from communities through the police department by threatening to sue departments and betting the police department will settle out of court. Although a police officer may have done nothing wrong and his actions were completely justified, the lawyer will twist any word in the officer's report to make it appear that an officer acted maliciously, violated policy, or was not trained sufficiently.

Here is a story of an officer I met who was sued, and the suit continued for several years:

The officer was dispatched for a domestic violence call. The parents made the call to the police department for assistance in controlling their mentally ill son. After the officer arrived at the residence, the parents told the officer their son had not taken his medication for several days and he threatened to kill himself and the parents. The parents also informed the officer that the son was diagnosed as a schizophrenic who demonstrated periodic acts of violence in the past. After the officer's backup, arrived they went to the rear bedroom where the son was staying. The officer spent several minutes talking to the subject, but he would not respond or acknowledge the officer's presence. The officers decided to go hands-on and cuff the subject to transport him to a medical facility. This engagement resulted in a four-minute fray that caused one officer to break his hand as the subject and officer fell onto a dresser drawer, and the suspect broke his arm in two places. Consequently, the parents sued the officers and department. The suit took three years to be resolved, during which time the officer who had broken his hand was told that the department wasn't going to represent him and that he would need to provide for his own defense. After two depositions and much litigation, the officer's department settled the case.

During those three years, the officers stated they were consumed with thoughts of the suit because they could not believe they were being sued for doing what any officer would have done, given the same set of circumstances. The officer who broke his hand said that the suit permeated his life, resulting in his separation from his wife and children, ending in a divorce.

Although it is common for people to threaten police officers with lawsuits in an attempt to intimidate an officer prior to or during an arrest or any other enforcement action, the person who sues will probably not be the person the officer expects to do so. That is why it is extremely important for the officer to write complete and comprehensive reports of all activities that could possibly result in a civil action. However, even if officers are very conscientious in report writing and continually educate themselves on the laws, it will not necessarily prevent one from being listed as a defendant in a lawsuit. And the worst-case scenario is when the police department separates itself from an officer in a lawsuit. Although this separation is a rare occurrence, it does happen and will result in added stress in an officer's life.

Reason Twenty-Five: The one-year wonder. The one-year wonder is an officer that gets acknowledgment for doing the same excellent job that other officers do, the difference being that one-year wonder's efforts always seem to get the kudos. Most of the time this "wonder boy" will be a Golden Boy who has won the favor of supervisory personnel because the wonder boy makes everything he does appear grandiose. In reality, the one-year wonder hasn't done anything that anyone else hasn't done.

A common story relating to this reason comes from a patrol officer:

The officer had been on the police force for three years and worked with a swing-shift squad that produced good, solid arrests. He was attempting to get into an investigative unit, when a new officer, a "one-year wonder" who had just finished probation, arrived on the squad. After a couple of months there was a posted opening for an investigative unit. When the officer inquired about the opening, he was told the position had been filled by the one-year wonder because he had been recognized for his high performance during his probationary period. The officer stated that his performance was as good as or better than the one-year wonder, but to no avail—the officer was passed over.

The one-year-wonder officer is just one of those things that happen in the police field. There are many reasons that will cause the one-year wonder to be picked for an assignment before more experienced officers. You need to understand that police work is part of a system that does not always operate fairly. Favoritism, nepotism, and cronyism are prevalent situations in a police department.

Reason Twenty-Six: "My job is the most important in this department." One of the ways police organizations are unique is in having different units within the police department (i.e., units for firearms training, vehicle training, defensive tactics, SWAT, Vice, and so on). Larger departments will have officers assigned specifically to these units full time. Many times officers assigned to these specialized units come to believe that their unit's work is the most important to the overall goal of the department.

This "my job is the most important" mentality is prevalent in large police departments, as this story demonstrates:

An officer, after completing his quarterly firearms training, was standing outside the door of the firearms meeting room listening to the firearms instructors talk about making the firearms course more difficult and implementing ground shooting along with other obstacle firearm training. The firearms instructors completed their meeting and exited the room when the officer approached the firearms instructor. Both had known each other and felt they could speak openly. The officer wanted to know why the firearms instructor wanted to increase the difficulty and frequency of the firearms qualification. The firearms instructor stated that he believed that the offic-

ers in the department were not competent enough and needed to shoot more frequently to become better marksmen/women. The officer replied that if the firearms training was increased along with all the other mandated training, officers would have less time on the street. The officer told the firearms instructor that to expect every officer to be as proficient as the firearms train-ers would be an unrealistic goal. And it appears the training officer working these specialized units wanted officers to be as proficient as the training officers. In addition, the officer pointed out that the training officers work-ing these units spend the majority of their time improving the unit's partic-ular skill and thus will naturally be more proficient in those areas than the other officers. The firearms instructor stated that liability is the issue when training involves firearms and therefore it is the most important. The officer pointed out that there have been more officers injured and killed in patrol vehicle accidents, so therefore more time should be spent doing defensive driver training. The officer arguing that officers should spend more time training for defensive driving was a full-time driver training officer.

This story demonstrates the mentality of many officers and supervi-sors that become assigned to these specialized units. The training offic-ers start to believe that their detail is the most important and that officers should become as good as the training officers assigned to the specialized units. This attitude is prevalent in police departments and should be understood when entering into the law enforcement profes-sion and wanting to test for a specialized unit. Officers begin to feel that they spend more time assigned to mandated training classes and have less time on the street doing their jobs.

Reason Twenty-Seven: Diversity? Sensitivity? Give me a break.
Diversity and sensitivity training is a fact of police work. The problem

with these types of touchy, feel-good classes is that so much of it has become nothing more than an old, tired joke to most police officers. The fundamental understanding of most officers is that police department administrations are pumping out mandated sensitivity seminars and ten-minute sensitivity videos covering every conceivable group. The objective is to give officers an understanding of different cultural and religious groups. Officers are expected to apply what they learn in these videos and possibly change their standard operating procedures in an attempt not to offend any specific group.

This story involves an officer who was mandated to view a ten-minute sensitivity video, and it was told by his supervisor:

The officer's department had mandated all officers watch a sensitivity video. The video suggested that officers having contact with a particular group should be sensitive to the religious requirements of that group and treat members of that group differently than they treat other citizens in the community. After the viewing of the video, the officer approached his supervisor and stated that he was a member of that religious group but of a different sect. The officer stated that he was offended by the stereotype portrayed in the video, because it did not mention the differences between the sects of the religious group viewed in the video. The supervisor replied to the officer, "Although I understand your feelings, the nature of the times is to expose officers to many different groups so that officers will have knowledge of these groups when contacting them in the field."

There is no way police officers can attempt to understand every religious and cultural group and sect of people in their communities. In addition, every smaller group within another larger group has its own cultural protocol. But here's the deal—if, for any reason, an officer is not sensitive enough with regard to a particular group, then the officer had better be prepared to justify his actions. The only way for officers to overcome the convoluted training of diversity and sensitivity is to treat all people—no matter their religious or cultural beliefs—with fair, firm, and consistent professionalism. Treating people with respect is the best defense against internal complaints for officers working in diverse communities. Officers should not attempt to identify any specific group, but to treat everyone fairly and respectfully, no matter their religious belief or culture.

Reason Twenty-Eight: "He was rude to me." This is a reason that involves a type of complaint that citizens will make about an officer because there is nothing else to complain about. Most people who use the "he was rude to me" complaint have received some type of enforcement action, for example, a citation or towing of their vehicle. Even when an officer is professional, some citizens will use the "he was rude to me" complaint for one of two reasons—either to get back at the officer, causing him as much grief as possible, or to make an attempt to squash the enforcement action taken by the officer.

The story told here demonstrates the "he was rude to me" complaint:

I was conducting radar at my usual place, stopping a driver doing 20 mph over the posted speed limit. I just had a feeling the driver was going to make a complaint on me, just by looking at the driver's countenance. So I acted as professionally and courteously as I possibly could, but the driver continued to argue with me. I let her talk for over three minutes and then told the driver I understood her frustration, but the citation needed to be signed. The driver continued to use profanity, flailing her arms out the driver's window at me. I just knew the complaint was coming, so I didn't say anything else and just held out the citation book for her to sign. Two weeks later I received a complaint from the internal affairs officer charging me with discourtesy (rudeness). My supervisor became extremely upset with me, because this was the third complaint he had to deal with in less than a week. The supervisor told me, "Just don't say anything to the drivers." I replied that would be considered "rude" and I would get a complaint for being short with citizens. Luckily the investigation found the charges "not sustained." That basically means that they could not find me either guilty or not guilty of the charge.

The "he was rude to me" charge is the staple of citizen complaints against police officers. The reality is that issuing a citation to a citizen does several things—it increases their insurance rates, imposes a fine, and usually makes the citizen later than they already are. So any time an officer issues a citation could be considered "rude." Of course, there are times when police officers are not professional and they are rude to citizens. Many citizens are aware—as are officers—that citizens can file complaints. These types of complaints are he said/she said and many of these investigations against an officer will be found not sustained, as opposed to "unfounded." The "not sustained" complaint is defined as when an officer may be guilty of the action being investigated, but there is not enough evidence to find the officer guilty. Thus the "not sustained" complaint is an extremely frustrating finding when officers have not violated any policy and were being totally professional. But because there are no independent witnesses, the officer will not be found innocent. Every officer will have the "he was rude to me" complaint filed on him, no matter how courteous or professional he is.

Reason Twenty-Nine: The supervisor who has lost touch. The supervisor who has lost touch is the most common complaint line officers have about police supervisors. Officers will label a supervisor with this "lost touch" reason when the supervisor makes comments that generalize officer behavior. For example, in the "he was rude to me" complaint, a supervisor who is upset that officers are receiving numerous complaints about discourtesy may state, "Just don't talk to them." The officers who hear this type of comment automatically believe that their supervisor has forgotten that if a citizen is going to complain, there is not anything an officer can do about it.

Elements of the previous reason are illustrated here to show how a police supervisor can lose touch:

A group of traffic officers stated that their lieutenant received several complaints regarding officer discourtesy. The complaints were all similar in nature, stating that officers were short with citizens on traffic stops. The officers reminded their immediate supervisor that they were directed not to argue or converse with the drivers and thus the citizen would have nothing to complain about. The supervisor who told the officers not to talk to the drivers told them to use common sense and act accordingly. The officers told the supervisor that they were in a lose-lose situation. The officers stated that there is no way of knowing when or how much to say to a driver who is upset and receiving a citation.

The above story is just one situation in which an officer will have to deal with a supervisor who has lost touch and has forgotten that there are situations that officers just can't win. There will be situations that will result in complaints by citizens, no matter what an officer does or says. Supervisors who have lost touch with line officers have forgotten about lose-lose situations. Complaints are part of doing the job of a police officer. If an officer has not generated a complaint, he is more than likely not doing anything. But the effects of complaints and how the supervisor handles them will be a major factor affecting the performance of officers. Supervisors who have lost touch will contribute to early burnout for line officers. The officers internalize the complaints, whether legitimate or not, thus causing stress that will manifest in officers' personal and professional lives. Mishandling of a complaint by a supervisor will magnify this situation.

Reason Thirty: "Back in the day, cops had more respect for the career." This saying is as old as police work itself. The adage is used by old, salty cops, comparing their motivations for becoming police officers to the motivations of newly hired police officers. The old-school police officers believe that their motivation for becoming a cop was based on a perspective of seeing the profession as a career and having a passion for helping people, whereas the new generation just sees police work as "a job." All new-generation police officers will confront the old versus new mentality. The reality is that cops nowadays face a much more litigious society, more convoluted laws, and are put in the middle of every type of domestic situation that one could imagine.

Many officers will witness this old versus new, better versus worst mentality. The following story is a typical example of the superior attitude that many officers will encounter:

I was at a police supervisory conference when one of the instructors passed out an article for the attending supervisors to read. The article was titled "The New vs. Old." We were instructed to read the article and discuss it with other supervisory personnel in the class. The article made comments about how new cops just didn't have the same passion for police work as the older generation of cops did. The group read and discussed it. Generally, the consensus of supervisors in the class agreed with the author's conclusion, which stated that police hired today didn't have the same passion and motivation that they had when they started police work over ten years ago. The fact is that the article was written over fifteen years ago, so the article was speaking about the officers in our classroom as the "new," not the officers being hired today. After this fact was revealed, the supervisors in the class did not have much to say—other than stating they still believed officers hired today are not of the same quality as when they themselves hired on.

The bottom line is this: No matter when an officer starts police work, the older officers will still believe that they are better cops than the present generation. The old versus new mentality is just another stereotype that officers of today have to live with until they become the old salty dogs, and then they will say how much better they are than the new generation of up-and-coming officers.

Reason Thirty-One: Cops are their own worst enemies. "Innocent until proven guilty" is the basic principle of our justice system and police work—right? Well, except when police officers become involved in an incident in which the officer's integrity or professionalism comes into question. Other cops will be the last ones to give another officer the benefit of the doubt.

The story relating this reason is as follows:

An officer had been dating a girl for just a few months when he and the girl went over to her house for the night. While there, he asked her if she had any cold water to drink, and she replied there was cold water in the refrigerator. The officer found a bottle of what appeared to be cold water. The next thing he knew he was in the hospital being treated for an overdose. The liquid in the bottle was apparently GHB, a drug that affects the central nervous system. GHB is colorless tasteless and odorless and can be added to beverages and ingested unknowingly. One of the popular reasons for using GHB is for a dietary supplement.

The officer suffered a tremendous blow to his reputation, as other officers in his department had made him out to be a drug user. The officer survived this incident and was able to regain some of his previous reputation, but he believes that there will always be a number of officers that will never accept that he was an innocent victim and ingested the GHB unknowingly.

The reason officers are so very quick to condemn other officers and to presume them guilty rather than innocent lies in the nature of police work. Many people officers come in contact with are guilty and are consequently found to be guilty in a court of law. The fact that cops are their own worst enemy is just another reality of the nature of a law enforcement career. Officers will come to realize and anticipate that other officers will generally not give a fellow officer the benefit of the doubt when accused of a violation, criminal or civil. Only when an officer finds himself in a precarious ethical situation will he realize how his other colleagues will presume his guilt based solely on rumor and hearsay before the facts are revealed.

Reason Thirty-Two: What thin blue line? The thin blue line, sometimes referred to as the code of silence among contemporary law enforcement officers, makes for good television, but does not hold true for today's modern police. Generally speaking, there is a subculture or mutual understanding among police officers but that is where it ends. Police officers, as a rule, do not cover up for each other or conspire to seek retribution on criminals that prey on our communities. The only place that an officer might benefit, and I emphasize *might*, is when an officer is stopped in his own personal vehicle and not issued a traffic citation—only because he is a cop. Nowadays many departments have electronic citations, and once the citation is written, there is no way to void it out. Therefore, most cops' wives, families, and friends will not benefit from knowing a police officer.

An illustration of this is in the following story:

An officer was pulled over in his own personal vehicle while on his way to the police station for work. A traffic officer pulled him over for driving 15 mph over the speed limit. Both officers worked for the same police department, but did not know each other, although the driver (officer) knew that the traffic officer had a relative who he did know, who worked in the same police department. The driver did not want to come right out and say that he was a cop, so he told the traffic officer that he knew one of his relatives who worked for the department. That reference opened the door for the traffic officer to inquire as to how the driver knew this relative. The driver told the traffic officer that he also was an officer for the department. The traffic officer told the driver, after he finished writing a citation, "Well, just go to court and tell them you're an officer, and they will probably reduce the citation to a lesser fine."

So much for the "thin blue line." The one change in policing that officers have noted in the last twenty years is that officers are not receiving "professional courtesy" when being stopped by other officers for minor traffic violations. Today, if an officer receives a citation from another officer, even if that officer works for the same department, it is not a surprise and most officers have come to accept that this is the fact of modern law enforcement.

Reason Thirty-Three: The cop who gets you involved in an internal investigation. Unlike most other professions in which employees are only responsible for their own actions, police officers are also required to be responsible for the actions of others. Police officers will be held liable for the actions of other officers and citizens throughout their careers.

The story that demonstrates this reason is as follows:

Two officers respond to a disturbance call involving a large male, described as intoxicated, standing outside of a local nightclub, yelling, and berating customers walking in the area. The officers arrived and made contact with the suspect. After several attempts to reason with him, he started to take an aggressive stance and the fight began. The officers were able to handcuff the suspect without injury to themselves or the suspect. During the confrontation, one of the officers became frustrated with the suspect's continual abusive language and punched the suspect while he was in handcuffs. The owner and manager of the nightclub witnessed the events and the officer punching the suspect. Although the manager made the initial call to the police, he also made a complaint on the officers for excessive force. The officer who punched the suspect was found sustained on a charge of using excessive force, and the other officer was found negligent for not intervening and separating the other officer from the suspect and failing to report the excessive force incident to his supervisor.

This type of incident illustrates that officers are responsible not only for their own actions, but also the actions of other officers. So for the individual who is considering law enforcement as a career, be aware and prepared to accept that police officers are held responsible for the actions and inaction of others.

Reason Thirty-Four: The essence of the job. Who are these people? Police officers are citizens, members of the community who are motivated and have obtained a certain level of education and have made the right decisions in life to be successful. Officers are individuals who contribute to their communities and have respect for the law. An officer's goal is to catch the "bad guy" and put him in jail. Officers spend the majority of their time contacting victims, interviewing suspects, and arresting criminals. The essence of the environment in which police officers work is negative. The majority of individuals contacted by the police are people who haven't made good decisions throughout their lives and will probably continue to make poor decisions for the rest of their lives.

The best story that depicts this reason is demonstrated in a call that I went on to check the welfare of a couple of children:

An anonymous neighbor made the call to the police about two children living in a residence who were not being cared for or supervised. When I arrived at the residence, the front door was open. Due to the nature of the call, I went into the residence to check on the children who had been reported inside. When I entered the small two-bedroom residence, I was immediately taken aback by a foul odor. I entered the kitchen area where there were dirty dishes stacked six inches high on the counter and the sink was filled with dishes caked with dried food. As I came within three feet of the kitchen counter, I notice a black coating covering the top portion of the plates. Much to my surprise, the black coating was a blanket of miniature flies. Just as my eyes focused on the insects, they lifted off the plates, forming a black cloud swarming throughout the residence. Exiting the kitchen, quickly, I continued to search for the children, entering the living area, where I observed dog feces scattered about the room. When entering the one and only bathroom, I saw the hot water heater resting on its side in the bathtub with electrical wiring exposed. The water heater appeared to be leaking and was obviously placed in the tub for the leaking water to drain. I left the vacant residence and began to walk back to my patrol vehicle, when an older lady approached me and asked if I had been looking for the children. I replied that I was, and she told me that she was the children's grandmother and she could take care of those kids better than their own mother. From twenty feet away, I could smell alcohol on her breath, which was probably because she had no front teeth to obstruct her alcohol-satu-rated breath. I told her that if she saw the children she should call us back. After taking another gulp of her 16-ounce Budweiser, she told me she would be sure to do that. As I drove off, I thought, "Who are these people?"

New officers who have never been exposed to these types of people or environments will have difficulty understanding these situations and working in this negative environment. The essence of police work is dealing with negative situations and tragic people.

Reason Thirty-Five: Different rules. Police officers give up certain rights afforded by the Constitution of the United States and its amendments. The degree of rights an officer gives up depends on the department policies and state statutes. The U.S. Supreme Court has stated that police officers are held to a higher standard regarding aggravating speech, and some state courts have set precedence that officers working cannot be listed as victims for certain crimes, that is, indecent exposure-type criminal offenses. State courts have also upheld department policies restricting where officers can work off duty.

The story illustrating this reason is about an officer who wanted to work as a valet, but the officer's department would not allow officers to work as valets:

The officer wanted to work for a hotel that had a valet service. The officer's department would not grant the officer's off-duty employment request, nor would the department give a reason for not allowing him to work for a valet service other than that it was against policy. The officer, at his own expense, took the department to court. The case went to court, and both the department representative and the officer's lawyer waited for the deposition of the presiding judge. The judge stated that if the department didn't want their officers to work for a valet service, then, "I guess, they shouldn't." The judge gave no other reason than that. The officer lost the case and the money paid for his attorney, but he didn't regret his decision to bring the department into court because he believed in his cause. The ironic part of this story is that the officer has now retired and is working as a valet.

Police officers will have many rules, regulations, and laws applied to their professional and personal lives. If an individual wants to be a police officer, he or she must consider that many things that an officer might want to do may be limited, if not forbidden, by department policies or state statues.

Reason Thirty-Six: "What have you done today?" For the most part, police work produces an intangible product, such as community security, which is difficult to measure. Generally, police officers defend their productivity or lack thereof by stating that police work can't measure crimes that have been prevented by officer presence. The intangible, immeasurable product argument that some administrators and officers have made in the past is slowly fading away and being rejected by the new generation of police administration. Thus, the new generation of police management is turning to new and innovative ways to monitor and measure police officer productivity. Some of these innovative ideas include tracking systems mounted in the patrol vehicle, cameras, and other effectiveness measurement methods include the use of statistical data sheets completed by each officer to measure each officer activity for the shift.

The following story reflects this trend of administrations attempting to measure productivity:

A captain assigned to a traffic unit conducted an interview with a local news reporter. The reporter asked if traffic officers had a quota to maintain an officer's minimum performance. The captain replied with an analogy that went something like this: "The local hamburger flipper must make so many hamburgers in an hour. If he can't maintain this minimum amount, he will lose his job. This same example is applied to our traffic officers—if they cannot write a minimum number of citations during a shift, they will not be performing at the standard set by the traffic bureau. Thus officers are required to perform at a level that is measured by the number of citations he writes.

Now, whether you agree with this analogy of comparing traffic officers with burger flippers is not the issue. The trend of police administrations is to hold officers accountable for their time in the field and produce measurable results. This new philosophy is where law enforcement is headed. In the future, if an officer is not able to produce the expected results, he will be held accountable.

Reason Thirty-Seven: It will take ten "that-a-boys" to make up for one "oh, shit." In this regard, police work is no different than other professions—there are rules, regulations, and guidelines to follow and failing to follow these procedures can result in disciplinary actions. If an officer makes a mistake in the field and this mistake is interpreted as a violation of police department policy, usually referred to as an "oh, shit," that one mistake can have a dramatic effect on his or her career or possibly prevent the officer from testing successfully for a specialized assignment. An officer who receives a "that-a-boy" is recognized by a supervisor for doing a good job. The "that-a-boy" can be a pat on the back or a letter of commendation for a job well done. The "oh, shit" is exactly that, something an officer did, or a decision he made, that resulted in an outcome that violated a rule, procedure, or policy. Many times the "oh, shit" is just the result of an officer forgetting something, for example, not completing paperwork or forgetting a court date.

The story I will relate here involves an officer who had an exceptional work history performance, but when it came to giving him discipline for an "oh, shit," the administration wouldn't think twice:

The officer had been working for the department for over ten years and never missed a court date generated by his arrests. In one year, he had more DUI arrests than any other officer in the state. The more arrests an officer makes, the more subpoenas issued; thus the subpoenaed officer will be required to report to court as a consequence of his arrests. Well, as the story goes, he missed one of the court dates and the district attorney's office sent a letter of delinquency to his commander. The commander, without hesitation, sent an order for the officer to be disciplined. Once the officer received the notice that he was going to be disciplined for failing to appear in court, he realized that he had forgotten that particular subpoena in his report box. But even so, he couldn't believe that the commander was so quick to discipline him for just this one incident.

The officer wrote a letter explaining the situation and also noted in the letter to the commander that he was the top producer of DUIs in the state. The commander stated that there is no excuse for an officer to miss a court date and that the officer will be held accountable, no matter what their arrest record is.

The officer's past performance had no weight in influencing the commander's decision. One of the most prevalent complaints of police officers is that their past performance is not a consideration when an officer makes a mistake. Officers usually say, "It doesn't matter what you did yesterday, only what you did today." A rule of thumb is that it will take ten "that-a-boys" to make up for one "oh, shit." Police work is a profession that requires officers to be versed in a number of legal situations. Officers are not going to be right in their decision 100 percent of the time. An officer may make ten good decisions, but rest assured, the one bad decision will be the one that gets the most attention.

Reason Thirty-Eight: "But I took all the classes." This reason shows that just because an officer is diligent and has a career plan doesn't necessarily mean that he will accomplish his professional goals. In order to test for a specialized unit, for example, K-9, traffic, narcotics, and so on, an officer will more than likely have to work as a patrol officer for a certain length of time. Usually police departments require patrol officers to work a minimum of two to four years prior to testing for these types of specialized assignments. Most officers will use this time to take in-service training classes or pay for seminars that will improve their chances of getting a specialized assignment. But specialized units do not always take the best or most qualified officers.

The best illustration of this reason is as follows:

An officer wanted to test for the traffic section and to operate a police motorcycle. The officer knew that he wanted this position even before he became a police officer, and knew there was a mandatory two-year period before he could apply for a position as a motor cop. He used the two-year waiting period and took every class that his department offered and paid for basic motor training outside of the department, attending the training on his days off. Additionally, the officer became the most proactive officer in investigating motor vehicle accidents and writing traffic enforcement citations. When the time came to test, there were eighteen candidates who applied for the police traffic section. After the traffic oral board met, he was rated as seventeenth of eighteen applicants. He found out later that there were officers who applied for the traffic positions and had not even taken one class to prepare themselves for the position, and several of the candidates did not even have motorcycle experience.

The reality is that police departments, as with private industries, reflect life and are not always fair to an individual. Although an officer may plan and prepare himself for a position, that doesn't mean he will get the position. Therefore, officers should always have an alternative plan and work toward both career goals simultaneously or many disappointments will await the prospective candidate.

Reason Thirty-Nine: "I blew out my knee." Injuries and police work go hand-in-hand. Most officers will suffer an injury during his or her career. Typical injuries include blown-out knees, back injuries, and/or a broken bone or two. Many of these injuries occur while chasing a "bad guy." Most police candidates who pursue a career in police work want a career that is physically challenging as well as professionally rewarding. Nevertheless, what many prospective candidates don't consider is the high potential for injury, and often these injuries are career-ending.

The story goes like this:

Since the officer could remember, all he wanted to do was to join the police department and become a cop. He joined his local agency at 21, completing the academy with ease. After only six months, while working on a graveyard shift, he responded to a petty larceny call at a local Stop & Shop. The dispatcher dispatched the description of the suspect as the officer was approaching the area. He saw the suspect walking across a field near the Stop & Shop. He was no more than ten yards into the foot pursuit when the officer stepped into a pothole and tore three ligaments in his knee. His knee injury was so severe that he was not able to maintain the minimum physical requirements of the job. He would only have 50 percent of the normal range of motion in his knee. Therefore, the department retrained him and assigned him to a desk job in the civilian section for half his original pay. The suspect that ran stole a six-pack of beer from the Stop & Shop.

The moral is that police officers will suffer from injuries. The majority of the incidents that result in officer injuries will not appear to justify the physical toll and the pain and suffering in the officer's life. So the police candidate should take heed that injuries will occur and hope that when they do, the injury will not end their career.

Reason Forty: The law. You are liable, not the judges or lawyers. Police officers are responsible for their actions and can be held liable for punitive damages suffered by those who can prove injuries were incurred as a result of the action of a police officer. On the other hand, lawyers and judges have an umbrella of immunity (absolute immunity). Generally, judges and lawyers cannot be held liable for their actions even if their actions are considered egregious. Many times officers will ask for the opinion of a local city attorney about some aspect of the law, but officers need to be aware that they will be held liable, not the attorney or judge.

A case that exemplifies this was heard by the U.S. Supreme Court, decided February 24, 2004. The Court found that Alcohol, Tobacco, and Firearms Officer Groh (Petitioner) wrote a search warrant that violated Ramirez's Fourth Amendment Rights. The gist of the case is stated below:

Groh v. Ramirez, Petitioner is not entitled to qualified immunity despite the constitutional violation because "It would be clear to a reasonable officer that his conduct was unlawful in the situation he confronted, Given that the particularity requirement is stated in the Constitution's text, no reasonable officer could believe that a warrant that did not comply with that requirement was valid. Moreover, because petitioner prepared the warrant, he may not argue that he reasonably relied on the magistrates' assurance that it contained an adequate description and was valid.

In other words, courts have found that immunity is viewed from a reasonable officer standard, not a reasonable lawyer standard (if there is such a thing as a reasonable lawyer—just a little cop humor). This is an aspect of law enforcement that many departments do not address with police officers. Therefore, it is up to the officer to inform himself about the liability of performing law enforcement actions. Additionally, there are state statutes that are stricter than federal law and require police in those states to be knowledgeable about those statutes and limitations that are placed on local law enforcement activities.

Reason Forty-One: The socialistic system—more work, same pay.
Police organizations are part of the civil service industry. Therefore, police departments follow civil service guidelines and have contracts, performance standards, and regulations for each and every employee to adhere to. There is no benefit or incentive to performing at a level beyond the minimum standard. The officer that outperforms other officers will be paid the same as if he were the worst, most incompetent officer on the force. The only incentive comes from the internal satisfaction that an individual feels, knowing that he has done a good job.

The story demonstrates how officers' yearly performance evaluations reflect the socialistic system:

My annual evaluation was due and without even an interview my supervisor handed me a completed yearly evaluation. The evaluation was short, generic, and said very little. After a day went by, my supervisor asked me if I wanted to add anything to it. I replied, "Yeah, how about the project that I created and designed for the station? How about all the hard work I've done throughout the year?" My supervisor replied, "Well, just write it up for me and I will see what I can do." After getting back the evaluation, it still said very little and I realized that the reward for hard work is the work itself.

The basic concept is to understand and realize that police work is not based on monetary compensation or recognition. A major factor for the police candidate to consider is whether he or she is motivated by money, platitudes, or a philosophic altruism. The only reward for good police work is the self-satisfaction an officer will get from performing above a set of minimum standards.

Reason Forty-Two: The supervisor who believes the citizen before he listens to you. Many times when a citizen files a complaint on an officer it will be sent to the officer's supervisor. The supervisor will usually receive the complaint via telephone or through a letter that the citizen has sent through the officer's chain of command. The supervisor who receives the complaint will usually investigate the problem—first, by contacting the citizen who made the complaint, and then the supervisor will contact the officer to get his side of the story.

The problem that occurs many times is that the supervisor will buy everything the citizen says without first speaking to the officer.

The following story illustrates the supervisor who believes the citizen before he will listen to the officer's side of the story, and it comes from an officer with several years of experience:

A citizen wrote a letter complaining about the actions of this officer and sent it through the officer's chain of command. The supervisor received the letter and began an informal investigation. The officer was called into the office and before the officer could get out a word the supervisor started to question the officer about his actions on a certain date and time and asked if he knew the contents of the complainant's letter. The officer had no idea what the supervisor was talking about, but the supervisor continued to question the officer regarding his actions toward the citizen. The supervisor's questioning continued with loaded accusations such as "When did you motion that you were going to pull the citizen out of his car window?" The officer said that he began to laugh at the questioning of the supervisor, knowing that he had never done such a thing to anybody. The result of the investigation was that the charge was unfounded, because there was a witness to the incident who could vouch for the officer behavior during the situation. Had the supervisor come straight out and asked the officer about the incident, the officer would have told the supervisor who to contact to substantiate his behavior toward the complainant.

Police work, just like other professions, has good and bad supervisory personnel. But seasoned officers are aware that a bad supervisor in law enforcement can cause serious injury to an officer's career and is another element that can add tremendous stress to an officer's life.

Reason Forty-Three: The off-duty caper—guilty. As I have mentioned in a previous reason, "Cops are their own worst enemies." It is important to note that off-duty capers are one of the most notorious for getting cops into trouble, resulting in discipline and, even worse, losing their careers. It is difficult for an off-duty officer not to act when witnessing criminal violations that could possibly injure someone.

One of the most common off-duty capers involves traffic incidents, and the story goes like this:

While driving home from work in his personal vehicle, the officer witnessed a driver weaving in and out of traffic and cutting off other drivers. When the reckless driver came to a stop at a traffic light, the officer approached the reckless driver, identified himself as a police officer, and brandished his badge. The driver exclaimed a number of profanities at the officer while exiting his vehicle and approaching the officer in an aggressive manner. The officer called in the incident earlier, and as other units arrived, so did his supervisor. The supervisor told the officer that he acted out of emotion and had not used good judgment when he approached the reckless driver. The officer agreed with his supervisor and stated that he did not think through the incident.

Most police officers will tell you that the best advice when witnessing an off-duty incident is to be a good witness. When officers, dressed in plain clothing become involved in off-duty situations and identify themselves as police officers, the incident usually escalates. Why? Studies have demonstrated that the uniform has a tremendous psychological impact on people to acquiesce to the authority that the uniform represents. Although many officers believe that they are required to act in an official capacity on or off duty, courts have established that off-duty officers are not liable when they do not take official action when witnessing a criminal act. The U.S. Supreme Court has ruled that off-duty officers do not have a legal obligation to respond to a criminal violation even when such violation could result in injury to another party.

Reason Forty-Four: The coroner's inquest, or shooting inquiry. The coroner's inquest is a hearing after an officer-involved shooting that resulted in a person's death. Other jurisdictions have different titles for the hearing, but the purpose is the same—to discover evidence surrounding the circumstances of an officer-involved shooting. Officers are subjected to numerous administrative and criminal court hearings after a shooting incident, when officers had to make a split-second decision to shoot or not. Other judicial processes include a civil suit, a criminal proceeding, and depositions.

Most of the hearings have significant psychological effects on the officers who are required to testify. The following story will give some insight into an officer's experience:

The officer was a former Marine and had four years on the police department. He was known for being a tough, no-nonsense officer. The officer became involved in a shooting incident that resulted in the death of a male subject. During the shooting inquest hearing, the officer recalled the shooting incident for the panel of citizens who reside over the hearing and vote on the findings of the incident. As the officer was on the stand recalling the incident, it was apparent that he was still traumatized by the incident. The officer had difficulty maintaining his composure and had to stop several times to collect himself. Some officers who have worked with him believe he was affected for years afterwards.

When officers are involved in traumatizing events, the criminal process does not allow them to forget the incident. In some cases, an incident requiring an officer to take someone's life will require the officer to recall the event for years. Most citizens, after suffering from a traumatic event, are encouraged to recall the event only once and then are allowed to try to forget it. But police officers are expected to remember all the facts and details of the event for years. Then the officer will be expected to testify and relive every detail of the event in front of dozens of people.

Reason Forty-Five: DUI and domestic violence. Unlike most other professions, if a police officer gets arrested for DUI or a domestic violence incident, the officer will most likely lose his job. In a DUI case, most departments will give the officer who has been arrested for DUI another chance, provided that he attends some type of alcohol counseling and if the DUI incident did not result in an accident resulting in an injury. But in a domestic violence case in which the officer (suspect) is found guilty, he will lose his career. There are two reasons why courts and police departments can't retain officers found guilty of domestic violence. First, the community and police department hold officers to a higher standard of behavior, and second, the U.S. Supreme Court has supported legislation stating that when an individual is arrested and convicted of battery involving domestic violence he or she loses the right to own a handgun. Therefore, the officer will lose his ability to carry and own a handgun.

The story told illustrates how serious the domestic violence law is, relating to police officers:

An officer with over ten years on the department was living with his girl-friend of two years. After a party one night, they returned home and a verbal argument ensued, resulting in the girlfriend calling one of her friends. This officer became agitated that she was on the phone and grabbed the base of the phone, resulting in the receiver end of the phone striking his girl-friend, leaving a red mark on her forehead. The girl she was talking with on the phone became concerned and called the police, because she knew that the couple had been in an argument. After the police arrived at the residence, the officer's girlfriend stated that he did not mean to strike her with the phone, but the responding police arrested the officer. After several months the officer's girlfriend contacted the district attorney and pleaded with him not to prosecute, but her pleas landed on deaf ears. The officer was convicted for domestic violence and subsequently terminated from the police department.

The above story demonstrates how serious the domestic violence laws are relating to police officers. There will be no second chance for officers. Officers who become involved in any type of activity that mandates arrest—for example, DUI or domestic violence—will risk losing their careers.

Reason Forty-Six: The crazy girlfriend. This reason ties into the previous one because men that like the excitement of a wild and crazy girlfriend will find themselves involved in a domestic violence situation. The above reason focuses solely on men because men tend to suffer the affects of this reason far more frequently than women will. Officers must be sensitive and cognizant to any red flags that a girl exhibits when establishing a relationship, such as if a girl has been involved in past relationships that have resulted in domestic violence or she has told stories of past relationship that resulted in her striking her previous boyfriends. This reason further demonstrates that police officers aren't going to get a second chance in a domestic violence situation. The risk of continuing a relationship with a crazy girlfriend is not worth the risk of putting a career in the hands of responding officers who will be mandated to take one of the two parties involved to jail.

The story I will tell here is one that I witnessed personally:

I went to work and while I was dressing in the locker room I saw a fellow officer who had a shiner that looked like something Mike Tyson would have been proud of. I asked the officer what had happened and he told me that his girlfriend had gotten upset and hit him in the face with a lamp. I asked him what he did after she hit him, and he replied that she always acted like that when she was upset. He also stated that she would pull his hair out and hit him for several minutes when she was upset. She told him she had always been involved in that type of physical confrontation with all her boyfriends. He also stated that he would just try to block her hands as she struck him. I told him that that was domestic violence, and he then replied that "that behavior was natural for her" and that she did not mean to hurt him.

Although the subject officer did not believe the acts of his girlfriend were abnormal, he was putting himself in a situation that could result in a domestic violence charge. As stated in this and the previous reason, the risk is too high for police officers being involved in any type of domestic problem with women who exhibit violent behavior.

Reason Forty-Seven: Internal investigations of police misconduct. Who said anything about being "fair"? Ninety-nine percent of police officers will be investigated for one thing or another during a twenty-five-year career. If you meet an officer who has not ever been investigated, either by their internal investigative unit or by their supervisor, the odds are that he's never worked the street for any amount of time or has never done anything closely related to police work. The following is a brief explanation of how most police departments' internal investigation unit works.

Like any other specialized unit on a police department, internal departmental investigators are expected to produce results. In today's environment, with the influence of civilian review boards, pressure of special interest groups and a police department's administration constantly putting pressure on internal investigators, often officers under investigation will find the internal investigative process unfair. Officers involved in internal investigations must understand that political pressures are a part of the system. These pressures are a fact and anyone who works or has worked for an internal investigation unit is lying if they say that politics does not factor into an investigation. The investigative process can be a long and drawn out procedure, so the cost of an investigation is significant. If, for example, an officer is being investigated and the investigation takes weeks or months to complete, the investigative unit has spent several thousand dollars of taxpayer (department) money. The investigators will have considerable pressure to find officers guilty—guilty of something—anything! If internal investigators find a charge against an officer not sustained after spending several days or months on an investigation, the administration will want to know why investigators invested that amount of time on a charge that couldn't be proven. There is also the factor of whom the officer knows. Simply stated, who you know plays a big part in the internal investigative process.

I will relate a supervisor experience to demonstrate the above facts:

The supervisor received a call from an internal investigating officer who informed him that he was being investigated for neglect of duty and various other violations of discourtesy involving the complainant. The supervisor recalled the complainant and the incident that had resulted in the complaint. The supervisor knew that the complainant was a life-long con artist and had spent the majority of his life in prison. The supervisor asked if the investigators had checked the veracity of the complainant's statements. The internal investigator assured the supervisor they checked out his story "leaving no stone unturned." The complainant told the investigator that the supervisor allegedly refused to take a report for the complainant about him being robbed of $30,000 and several thousand dollars in camera equipment. In addition, the investigator told the supervisor that the complainant went to another substation after contacting him to report the incident. At *that time the investigator admitted that the complainant had already begun to change his original story, as the complainant told another officer that only $6,000 in cash was taken from him. After the complainant was successful in conning another officer into taking a false report, he went to the internal affair's unit. There, the complainant told the investigators that he had first reported $30,000 was taken and then recanted his story to the second officer. He then admitted to the internal investigator that not even $6,000 was taken, but he wanted to file a complaint on the supervisor for refusing to take the initial report. The supervisor pointed out to the investigator that the complainant had admitted he had committed a crime to the investigator (filing a false police report).*

The supervisor asked the investigator if the history of the complainant had been checked as had been done during the initial contact. The investigator told the supervisor that they had checked out the complainant completely, discovering he had worked for the Oprah Winfrey show. The supervisor told the investigator that the complainant had a criminal history that would have made Billy the Kid envious. For example, the complainant had spent two-thirds of his life in prison for bank robbery, grand larceny, several petty larcenies, defrauding inn keepers, and so on. Basically the guy was a con artist who would have used any police report to establish that he had money, to get a free meal, or anything else he could think of. After the supervisor pointed out these facts, relating to the complainant continually changing his story and never establishing that he had $1 much less $30,000, the investigators became so embarrassed, the internal complaint was dropped before it was started.

The above story demonstrates that there is considerable pressure on internal investigators to investigate charges against police officers. Most police departments do not give specialized training to internal investigators and the result is poor investigations and a waste of departmental resources. Additionally, one of the largest misconceptions that most individuals have regarding police internal investigations is that the investigation is governed by the rule of due process. It isn't. For example, officers under investigation do not have a right to confront their accusers or review evidence brought against them. The only level of evidence needed to find an officer guilty of a charge is that of preponderance of the evidence, not the stringent standard of due process requiring reasonable doubt.

Reason Forty-Eight: "I pay your salary." This reason is another one of those one-liners people use in an attempt to intimidate a police officer. Although the "I pay your salary" statement has become a cliché, officers still hear it from time to time. When an officer hears this statement from a citizen, it automatically puts the officer on the defensive. Officers learn to handle this comment, as they do most other comments, and just learn to ignore it.

One of the best stories that demonstrate this reason was told by a traffic officer:

While working traffic control he conducted a traffic stop on a driver who was extremely agitated. The driver expressed his displeasure by attempting to get under the officer's skin saying, "Why did you pick me out of everyone else? Don't you know 'I pay your salary'?" The officer, while still writing the citation, didn't miss a beat and replied, "Excuse me, sir, but where do you work?" and the driver replied at a local supermarket. The officer then stated, "Well, I guess we are even then, because I shop there—therefore, I pay your salary too."

These one-liners are used for one of two reasons. The first is to vent frustrations on the officer, because no one likes to admit that they have done something wrong, and the second is to attempt to get under the officer's skin, hoping that the officer may say something that can be used to file a complaint against the officer. Most officers realize that the best policy is not to acknowledge such comments, because any response by an officer to such statements will appear as unsympathetic or rude.

Reason Forty-Nine: The Civilian Review Board. The Civilian Review Board has become a popular forum for local police departments. Usually the board's purpose is to review internal investigations conducted by police departments and is an alternative avenue for citizens to file complaints against officers. There are a number of ways in which review boards function that will not be discussed in this book—but the point is that a review board is another process to be used in reviewing an officer's actions. An officer usually acts and reacts based on the information and training that he has had, and the decision to act is done quickly without time for deliberation. But review boards have days if not weeks to review the actions of the officer and then make a determination as to whether the officer's actions were appropriate for the situation.

The story told here is related to an internal investigation that a police department conducted on one of its officers and how the review board responded:

The officer was charged with an internal complaint generated by a citizen claiming that the officer failed to take a report when the situation required the officer to do so. The officer was charged internally with neglect of duty. The police internal investigators exonerated the officers on all charges. The citizen appealed the decision to the Civilian Review Board. The board found the department's investigation to be inadequate and incomplete. The result of the board's review put pressure on the department, and thus the case was reopened. Consequently, the officer was subjected to another investigation in which he was found sustained on the initial charges.

Whether the review board was correct in reversing the decision of the internal investigation is not the issue. The issue is that officers are subjected to a number of review processes. Although the above story demonstrates a double-jeopardy situation, police officers involved in internal investigations are not protected by due process. Review boards and other administrative processes review an officer's decisions—decisions that he had sometimes only seconds to make. Therefore, any police candidate wanting to pursue a career in police work should realize that officers' decisions will be reviewed constantly throughout their career.

Reason Fifty: "Well, I can't work there now!" Police work and the ability to arrest people can have dramatic effects on the lives of others. For example, an arrest for a crime, such as domestic violence, DUI, handgun violation, or even a traffic violation can prevent an individual from pursuing a career in law enforcement. Police officers working in the field will come in contact with relatives of other officers in their department. Officers are sometimes placed in a situation in which they must arrest a family member who might be pursuing a career in the same department that an officer works for.

This arrest situation can cause hard feelings between officers who are working for the same department, as the following story explains:

A police supervisor was working swing-shift and was requested by his officers to assist in a burglary that involved a district attorney's son and another juvenile, who was the son of a police lieutenant in the same depart-

ment as the responding supervisor. *The lieutenant was assigned to a specialized detail, a detail that the supervisor wanted to transfer too. After the supervisor responded, he had to make the decision to arrest the two juveniles. The lieutenant arrived at the scene and was visibly upset at the supervisor's decision to arrest his son. The lieutenant told the supervisor that this would end any chance of his son testing and becoming a police officer for the department. And of course, it would end any chance of the supervisor being assigned to his detail.*

This situation is a perfect example of when the supervisor had to make the right decision, but that decision, would most likely result in the supervisor not being able to work for that specialized unit. As with most of these 101 reasons listed, this is one that demonstrates how many political pitfalls there are when working as a police officer.

Reason Fifty-One: The negativity of the job is the essence of the job. Most prospective police candidates who are interested in police work don't thoroughly understand the essence of a career in law enforcement, much less the essence of police work. Police work, by its nature, deals with people in stressful circumstances. Officers are not called to situations where there is no problem and everyone is happy to see them. After a police officer clears from a dispatched call, one of three responses is exhibited by the subjects involved in the event. One possible response, involving two individuals, will be that one person is upset at the officer's decision and the other is pleased. A second response is that both parties are upset at the decision of the officer. The third and rarest situation is when both parties are pleased with the results of the actions of the officer.

The story told here involves an officer responding to a typical domestic violence call:

An officer arrived at a residence where two parties were visibly upset at each other. The officer conducted an investigation and determined that the female committed a battery on the male during an argument. The officer explained that the domestic violence law requires that the person committing the battery must be arrested, and thus the officer arrested the female. The male became extremely angry at the arresting officer and began to scream at the officer, telling the officer that he had no right butting into their lives. The officer told the male that he did not just drive by his home and decide to invite himself into their lives. The officer reminded the male that he called the police, and when he did that, he made the decision to have the police intrude into their lives.

The nature of police work requires officers to butt into other people's lives and make decisions that people will not be pleased with. Police work deals with people at their worst, and this constant negativity can have dramatic effects on an officer's private life. To understand the essence of police work is to be prepared for being viewed as a negative element that is forced into the lives of others, a necessary evil.

Reason Fifty-Two: "What have I accomplished in the last twelve to fifteen years?" Many officers will start to reflect over their careers at the mid point which tends to be between twelve to fifteen years. At this point, an officer begins to look back at his career and evaluate what he has accomplished since his academy days.

The story told here is from a fourteen-year veteran who has had a diverse career working in three specialized units:

As an officer I have been fortunate, having worked in a variety of specialized units. Thinking back after all these years, I can't say that I've been as productive as I would have liked. I think about retirement on a weekly basis and believe this is because of the constant negativity. This negative environment has had a tremendous impact on my personal life. I remember that I had a positive attitude toward people as a new officer and I usually thought the best of people. But now the negative elements of the job seem to affect me more now then it ever has. I haven't pursued any diversions or alternative activities separate from the job. Knowing what I know now, I would not have chosen this career because of the toll that it has had on my personal life. I don't think anything can prepare a person for the daily stresses that police work puts on your friends and family.

Many people have second thoughts about their choice of career, but there is no doubt that police work is one profession that will have a dramatic effect on a person's personality, friends, and family. Police work will change an officer's view of people and society in general. As stated previously in an earlier reason, "the essence of the job is negative."

Reason Fifty-Three: The indelible image—it's there for life. Police officers will see things that the average citizen will never experience. These incidents range from homicides and suicides to fatal traffic accidents. Many of these events will leave an image in the officer's mind that he will carry for the rest of his life.

This story was from a patrol officer who had twelve years of experience, and it relays his indelible image:

The officer was headed in for the shift. When he was one block from the station house, he observed several people in the middle of the street. When he approached the group, several of the citizens started to wave at him in an attempt to get his attention. The officer blocked off the traffic lane, believing that an auto accident had occurred. As the officer walked toward the crowd, he saw a young lady lying in the middle of the traffic lane. He approached her from the front. Her eyes were wide open, and she appeared to be gasping for breath. He thought she didn't look seriously injured, but then he saw that a bus had hit her and stopped fifty feet down the travel lane. When the officer bent down to observe her injuries, he saw that she had been run over by the bus's rear wheels, causing injuries to the base of her neck down to the lower back. Her entire back had been broken open, exposing her rib cage. Every rib had been broken away from the base of her spine. Her organs, although connected, were exposed, lying on the asphalt. He then glanced to her face, hoping that she was in shock and numb. He felt totally helpless to help her. The image of her countenance and her injuries stayed with him for weeks after the incident. He was unable sleep without seeing her face. He said that he has never forgotten her or the image of the fatal injuries she suffered.

Police officers will always be exposed to the worst incidents and many of these events will create images that will be with the officers for the rest of their lives. Although some callousness develops in police officers because of the consistent number of gory scenes that officers respond to, officers will still confront situations that will resonate with them on a personal level.

Reason Fifty-Four: "Hey, do you remember me?" This is a common event and usually happens when an officer is off duty, in civilian clothing, and has come into contact with an individual whom he doesn't want to remember. But the person remembers the officer. This situation can be very dangerous, because the officer doesn't know if this person was a victim he helped or a suspect he arrested and was subsequently sent to prison for twenty years.

The story comes from an officer who worked in a number of rough areas in a large city:

I was with my family and out for a quiet dinner. As we were waiting for a table, a large male approached me from the rear and asked, "Hey, do you remember me?" I turned and faced the male subject. I didn't remember who this subject was, and as my mind raced, thinking "Did I arrest this guy or is he just a friend of a friend?" Seconds passed and the subject didn't say anything else—he just stared at me. I replied, "No, no I don't—should I remember you?" The subject then just walked out of the restaurant, and I had to look over my shoulder for the rest of the night.

This is a fact of life in police work. Officers arrest many people and most of them the officer will not remember—but you can bet they will remember the officer who arrested them. These situations will occur throughout an officer's career, and most of the time nothing will come of it. But having a healthy paranoia is better than a punch to the back of the head.

Reason Fifty-Five: Getting stopped by—and being the victim of—a rude cop. Police officers are like other professionals—they want to be perceived as professional. When an officer witnesses another officer acting in an unprofessional manner, it is embarrassing. When an officer acts unprofessionally, other officers realize that the unprofessional behavior carries exponentially throughout the profession. A unique phenomenon relating to police work and how other officers subconsciously identify themselves with the unprofessional acts of other officers is demonstrated when officers become embarrassed by the actions of other officers.

The story that relates to this reason goes like this:

An officer was driving home late one night with his wife, in his personal vehicle. The officer was just a couple of blocks from his house when he slowly made a right turn, failing to stop at a stop sign. As the officer was in the middle of the right turn, he noticed a police vehicle several yards away. After completing the turn he said to his wife, "That's a cop, and I failed to come to a complete stop at the stop sign." Just after he made the statement, the officer on patrol activated his lights, pulling over the off-duty officer and his wife. The officer approached the driver and without any word spoken by the driver, started yelling "DO YOU KNOW WHAT YOU DID? YOU ALMOST HIT ME AND DO YOU KNOW WHAT THAT MEANS—YOU GO TO JAIL." The officer replied with a calm tone, "Yes sir, I ran the stop sign—sorry about that." The patrol officer then told the driver to give him his license and paperwork. When the driver opened his wallet, the patrol officer saw the police identification. The patrol officer then rudely asked, "What is that, a security ID?" The driver replied, "No, it's my police supervisor identification." The patrol officer's tone immediately changed as he started to mumble and stammer, saying, "Why didn't you say something?" The driver replied, "You didn't give me a chance." The patrol officer then told the driver to have a nice day. He appeared to be extremely embarrassed and quickly left in his patrol vehicle. The driver stated to his wife that he was embarrassed because the officer was representing his profession and his behavior was and is a refection on him and his profession.

This is an example of how officers will witness the acts of fellow officers and realize that other people's bad experiences with the police do reflect on them. No matter how committed to performing their duty in a professional manner officers are, officers unconsciously internalize the unprofessional actions of other officers. This internalization can add to officers' frustrations when they realize that citizens will generalize one bad experience to all officers.

Reason Fifty-Six: "What am I doing here?" No matter how professional or efficient a police officer is at doing his job, there will come a time in that officer's career when he feels his efforts are futile.

This reason was illustrated by a police officer who had seven years of law enforcement experience when he told of how he started to feel his efforts were in vain after an arrest he made:

The officer was working with a team of officers to catch a burglar suspect who was active in the area. The suspect had been identified and was a known burglar with an arrest record as long as Baby Face Nelson. The suspect evaded the police on several occasions in vehicle pursuits, but was not visually identified at the crime scenes. During the crimes, the suspect left several burglary tools at the scenes and the police had an informant who was giving them good intelligence. The officer wrote up a search warrant for the suspect's residence, resulting in the recovery of items taken in the burglaries.

After the suspect was in jail for a week, the district attorney released the suspect, stating there was not enough evidence to hold the suspect. After a week the burglaries resumed. The officers, having spent months on tracking the suspect, felt that all the work they did was wasted and that they had to start from scratch. The officer thought to himself, "What am I doing here?"

Police work can be extremely frustrating work. There are many times that an officer will know he has the right suspect, but he is unable to make an arrest because of the circumstances, or the district attorney will not prosecute for one of many reasons that the officer will not believe to be justified. Acceptance and understanding are virtues that must be developed by police officers. Frustration will be a large part of the job and is intrinsic to a career in law enforcement.

Reason Fifty-Seven: "Do you know Bob, John, etc.?" This reason is another one of those questions an officer will get when a driver is attempting to avoid a citation. The "do you know" is a subtle way of trying to make a personal connection with an officer who has stopped the driver because of a traffic violation.

The story relating to this reason comes from a traffic officer I met:

The officer stopped a driver for a minor traffic violation and was standing next to the driver's side window, writing a citation to the driver. The driver continued to ask the officer if he knew other officers in the department, asking, "Hey, do you know Bob?" as the officer responded in the negative. After dropping five other names, the driver mentioned an officer's name that he did know. The officer told the driver that he didn't know any of those officers he mentioned, and after handing the citation to the driver, the officer replied that he did know the last officer he spoke of and that the officer had slept with his soon-to-be ex-wife. Then there was a long silence, the driver drove off, and the officer went back to work.

Officers will hear every excuse imaginable and citizens will make every effort to get out of a traffic citation. Police officers will be required to write traffic citations to individuals who are friends or relatives of other officers in the same department where they work. These situations can cause friction between officers, as mentioned in other reasons. Officers should not expect nepotism or cronyism from other officers.

Reason Fifty-Eight: Leaving a mark. Motivated police officers, like other individuals in demanding professions, want to leave their mark. Basically a mark is something that will identify the officer with a particular unit or department policy—creating something so that the officer can say "I did that." The "leaving a mark" reason—sometimes referred to as the "immortality complex"—can lead to bad policy and/or a conflict from the creating officer wanting to be recognized at the cost of the overall department goal.

The story that goes with this reason was told by an officer who had considerable rank in a medium-sized department:

A senior supervisor in his department developed a program to address gang activities in a local gang-active neighborhood. The program was initiated and successful in reducing gang activities for a limited period of time. Due to the initial success of the program, it was named after the supervisor who had created the program. The supervisor began to be recognized for the program's success. But after several months, the gang members discovered the program's tactics and began to change their own modus operandi. The program had a specific design. As the gang members changed their tactics, the program needed to be changed to adjust to a new set of circumstances, and most of the officers who executed the enforcement activities realized this and thus requested changes to the program. The supervisor who created the program identified strongly with the program and began to be recognized for the program's initial success. The supervisor and creator would not allow any changes made to the program. Although crime analysis demonstrated that the program was losing its effectiveness, the supervisor would not abandon his creation. The result of the supervisor wanting to leave his mark was a demoralization of the officer responsible for executing the program.

Law enforcement is no different than other professions in that there are a variety of personalities. There will be situations in which an officer wants notoriety at the cost of the overall goal.

Although the basic concept of police work has always been the same, that is, to catch the "bad guy," law enforcement tactics are forever changing. Officers must be able to change quickly and adapt to these changes. Officers must not become ensconced in a particular system or way of thinking or they will fail to be effective in meeting the needs of their communities. If recognition is what you desire, police work is not a profession that would be conducive for achieving that goal.

Reason Fifty-Nine: "I'm a cop." "I don't care." Many people think there is a professional connection between police officers—an *esprit de corps*. But officers will come to realize that there is not an omnipresent bond in the law enforcement community between police officers. Off-duty officers will come in contact with an on-duty officer who couldn't care less about who they are or what they do. There aren't many cops who don't have a story of how poorly they have been treated by their fellow law enforcement "brothers." When an off-duty officer has a negative incident with an on-duty officer, it is an eye-opening and extremely disappointing event.

The stories that relate to this reason are numerous. I will relate a story that represents a situation when an off-duty officer encounters an on-duty officer. It's one to which most officers will be able to relate:

An officer, while driving to work in his personal vehicle and dressed in his uniform, was traveling in the opposite direction of a fellow officer who was working in a marked patrol unit, but for an adjacent jurisdictional department. The officer in the marked unit passed the officer traveling to work. The patrol officer turned around and stopped the other officer. After having been stopped by the patrol officer, the off-duty officer exited his vehicle, deliberately holding his hands above his waist to demonstrate that he was armed and in uniform. The patrol officer approached the uniformed officer, never acknowledging him as a fellow officer. Then the patrol officer began to ask why he turned his bright lights on when he was approaching from the opposite direction. The other officer replied that he turned his lights from high to low when he saw the patrolman approaching. The patrol officer continued to be abrupt, not listening or acknowledging him as a fellow officer, and just kept repeating his initial question. The officer who was stopped realized that the patrol officer was not going to treat him as a fellow professional. The off-duty officer just apologized for the misunderstanding. Then the patrol officer asked for the off-duty officer's license and registration.

Although most people think there is a common bond between police officers, experience will dictate otherwise. Situations involving off-duty and on-duty officers will no doubt prompt an officer to have an introspective look at himself and how he behaves when confronted with a similar incident.

Reason Sixty: The bait and switch. This is a situation that has become popular and has cost many officers their jobs. "The bait and switch" is used by fellow officers or ex-officers. The motivation for the bait and switch is to use the system to gain some type of financial or positional advantage. Officers who attempt the bait and switch are always searching for a situation involving a fellow officer—a situation that will provide fertile ground to bait an on-duty officer into acting contrary to his nature, actions that violate department policy or a person's civil rights.

The individual who is baiting an officer has the knowledge of police procedures and protocol and can manipulate the situation to give the perception that his rights were violated or he has witnessed an officer acting contrary to department policies.

The story that demonstrates the bait and switch goes like this:

While performing their duties, two officers were assigned to a downtown rally. The rally was briefed to be peaceful and have few if any confrontational participants. During the rally, an off-duty officer working for the same department as the officers assigned to the demonstration, confronted the two officers on the police line. The off-duty officer, acting as one of the participants of the rally, aggressively approached the two officers and began to yell antipolice sentiments. The officers did not know or recognize the off-duty officer. As the off-duty officer continued to create a disturbance, the two officers calmly requested him to move along. The off-duty officer-participant continued his disruptive behavior. After several minutes other officers started to arrive due to the disturbance. The off-duty officer realized that the officers were not going to move him along or react to his disruptive actions. The off-duty officer then identified himself to the officers and stated he just wanted to see how they would react. The off-duty officer then walked off, laughing.

The bait and switch is a fact of modern police work and there will always be individuals, whether police officers or citizens, who will attempt to bait an officer into acting in a manner that is contrary to an officer's nature. This bait technique can also be used to manipulate an officer to act contrary to a department policy, which will also result in disciplinary action for the officer—and the pseudo-victim can use this situation to file a lawsuit.

Reason Sixty-One: The incompetent attorney. Law enforcement officers and attorneys are forever professionally tied together. Police officers work and submit criminal cases to attorneys representing the people of the jurisdictions that officers are sworn to protect. Generally speaking, these city and county attorneys are neophytes. As a rule, talented public attorneys will make the move to private practice quickly. Thus, when officers attempt to get legal guidance or testify in court, they must endure the learning curve of inexperienced counsel.

The following story demonstrates this frustrating issue:

An officer in the field responded to a call involving two agitated parties, both of whom claimed to have rights to a child. The male half of the couple claimed to have the rights to the child and proceeded to show court documentation stating his custodial rights for the child. The female half also had documentation of similar weight, claiming the same jurisdictional position. The officer arriving on the call interviewed both parties and read all the documentation related to the issue. The officer, unable to make a determination regarding the convoluted documentation, made a call to the on-call city attorney. After relating the facts of the situation, the officer requested guidance from the attorney. The city attorney spoke to the officer for twenty minutes over the phone. Every other minute, the attorney would argue the point for the female half and then spend the next minute arguing the validity of the male's documentation. When the attorney finished speaking to the officer, the officer asked, "Give me the bottom line—who has the legal ground, so I don't find myself in a lawsuit?" The attorney stated, "Well, I don't know—do what you think is right." The officer, frustrated, replied, "That's why I called you!"

The bottom line for police officers is to realize that attorneys are paid to argue points and police officers are paid to make decisions. Attorneys can spend hours, days, or weeks contemplating a decision on what to do or how to avoid making a decision. Police are paid and trained to act and make quick decisions. This dichotomy is one of the most aggravating situations that officer faces. The one thing that officers forget is to do what they think is right with the amount of information they have at the time.

Reason Sixty-Two: The judge who sides with the defendant. Officers will find frustration with the bench as well as attorneys. Officers can spend weeks or months working on a case and have a judge throw out much of the officer's work, if not all the evidence gathered during a hard-fought case. This situation also occurs with minor incidents such as traffic violations.

The story told here involves an officer, a minor traffic citation, and a placating judge:

An officer was subpoenaed to traffic court for a case involving a motorist running a red light. The officer just finished working the graveyard shift and knew he would be one of the last cases called due to the minor nature of the incident. After several hours the judge called the officer and defendant, asking how the defendant pled. The defendant pled not guilty and then went on to state how the officer could not have seen him run a red light. Then the officer was called to testify to the facts of the violation. After hearing both sides, the judge stated that since he was not there and didn't know the officer, he would find for the defendant. The officer responded to the judge's decision, asking, "What does knowing me have to do with the defendant running a red light?" The judge, realizing what he had said, ignored the officer's statement and then called for the next case. The officer just walked out of the courtroom shaking his head.

Judges are no different than anyone else—they have biases. Therefore, the best way for an officer to handle placating judges and the poor decisions they make is to do what the officer knows is legal and right. Officers must realize that their job ends after the paperwork has been submitted to the court. The attorneys and judges have the responsibility to ensure that justice is carried out.

Reason Sixty-Three: "You might be right, but you're wrong." Simply stated, officers are expected to avoid situations that will put them in compromising situations. This reason applies mainly to an off-duty officer who becomes involved in an incident requiring on-duty officers to respond. The responding officers verbally or nonverbally communicate that they hold the off-duty officer responsible for creating and escalating an incident that requires police response. In addition, the off-duty officer's actions could result in departmental disciplinary action against the off-duty officer if such actions were scrutinized. But if a citizen were to react in the same manner, there would be no repercussions regarding the incident.

The following story demonstrates how this reason will apply to police officers:

When arriving home in his personal vehicle after work, the officer witnessed several juveniles running away from his home. The officer observed the juveniles enter a vehicle and drive off. At the same time he noticed that one of his house windows had been damaged. The officer followed the subjects and called the local police dispatchers to inform them of the situation on his mobile phone. After several miles, the juveniles realized that the officer was following them in his personal vehicle, and they started to drive recklessly through the neighborhood, attempting to evade the officer. The officer realized this was a dangerous situation, and he stopped following the subjects. After a few minutes the officer started to return home on a major street, and just by luck, he saw the subjects stopped at the same traffic light, three vehicles up from his vehicle. The officer exited his vehicle and walked up to the subjects' vehicle. The officer sternly ordered the subjects out of the vehicle. The subjects realized that he was the owner of the home where they had broken the window, and they refused to exit their vehicle. Then the officer started to knock on the driver's side window, breaking the juveniles' driver side window. The juveniles then exited the vehicle. All of the subjects and the officer waited for the local police to arrive. After the police arrived, the juveniles stated that the officer had assaulted them. After the responding police officers spoke with the juveniles, they went to speak to the officer involved. The supervisor who arrived on the scene contacted the off-duty officer involved and told him, "You might be right, but you're wrong."

Basically, what the supervisor told the (victim) off-duty officer was that no matter what happens, the officer involved will be judged by the outcome of the event, good or bad. Police officers are held to a higher standard, and sometimes that standard requires officers to be victims because if an incident turns bad he will be the one held responsible.

Reason Sixty-Four: "Why didn't you shoot the gun out of his hand?" Among other statements, this usually leaves police officers speechless. Situations that have inspired citizens to ask, "Why didn't the cop shoot the gun out of his hand?" have been fueled by a police drama television series. The fact is that it is hard enough to hit a stationary target under pressure, much less a handgun out of someone's hand, when that someone has the ability to shoot back at the officer.

The following story is from an officer who was asked this same question:

The officer was taking a class at the local community college. During the class, the topic of gun control and police fatal shootings became the focus of the conversation. The officer was surprised by the number of students who wondered why police officers didn't just shoot dangerous weapons out of the hands of people, as opposed to shooting and killing them. The officer attempted to explain how difficult it is just to be accurate enough to hit a person's center mass, much less shooting a moving target that's the size of a stapler out of someone's hand. The students responded to the officer, suggesting that police officers should become better shots and spend more time practicing. The officer became frustrated with his fellow students and said, "Well, why don't criminals shoot the guns out of the police officers' hands and then they wouldn't get shot!"

Television has had an impact on police stereotypes. The officers will come in contact with many individuals who believe that television is an accurate depiction of police work, that the "big screen" is a reflection of reality. Officers will experience frustration when trying to explain the actions or inaction of officers reported in the news, but this is the life of a police officer.

Reason Sixty-Five: There are always strings attached. A popular misconception about police officers is that they never have to pay for food or drinks. This is not always the case, and now more places charge on-duty officers full price for services rendered—although there are a few places that provide complementary food and coffee to police and firefighters. Experienced officers realize that nothing in life is free and there are always strings attached to these complementary services. Most officers usually give a tip that will cover the cost of services rendered, and if they don't, they should.

The following story illustrates the type of string that can be attached to a free service:

After eating at a local restaurant, the officer was about to leave the tip and exit the establishment. The manager approached the officer and told him that they had been robbed earlier in the week and wondered why the police had been so slow in responding to his establishment. The officer hadn't heard of the robbery and asked what had happened and if anyone was hurt during the event. The manager said that no one was injured—just shaken up—after the incident. The manager said that he gave officers complementary meals with the hope that they would patrol his establishment on a regular basis. The officer responded that there is no guarantee that such patrol action would occur and there were many businesses in the area that had similar problems. The manager was upset by the response and said that from now on he would charge officers half price for their meals. The officer told the manager that he should charge the full rate and know that he would still give the manager whatever service he could to meet his needs, but this is no guarantee that his establishment would not be the victim of criminal activities.

Complementary meals and drinks that businesses give to officers come with a price: there are always strings attached. Officers should be aware of such expectations and act accordingly. Nothing is free and this includes police services.

Reason Sixty-Six: Quasi-military, no room for creativity. Police academies, police departments, and police organizational structures are quasi military by nature. Although police work has changed, becoming more efficient, the changes are slow in developing. Creative police officers usually become extremely frustrated when they develop programs or procedures that would be an improvement on current practices, because new ideas face resistance from established ideologies.

A contemporary story that demonstrates this issue involves the Taser:

The Taser has been shown to reduce injuries and liability damages to police departments by millions of dollars. An officer who became involved in attempting to bring this technology to his department was told that the development of this technology was not proven and needed to be tested over time. The officer had written up a comprehensive study and documented the use of the Taser over the previous ten years, demonstrating the effectiveness of the device. The administration agreed with the officer that such technology would be an effective tool, but wanted to table the issue, placing it in a "wait and see" mode. The officer became frustrated with the administration, but continued to document and provide strong arguments for the implementation of the device. Two years later, his department developed a testing program for the Taser.

Change involving police organizations is slow, new ideas and concepts are usually resisted because many administrators do not want change and these dinosaurs do not move quickly. Officers who are creative and like to question the status quo will become frustrated with police work and the resistance faced when developing new programs. As a result, creative officers become detached and disillusioned when their efforts are not developed or supported.

Reason Sixty-Seven: It's a numbers game. Police work and police officers are like any other business and employees and they are expected to produce results. Although a considerable amount of what police organizations produce is an intangible product, contemporary police administrators are always trying to implement a new way of holding officers accountable for their time. These new ways of holding officers accountable are usually implemented in a statistical format. Most of these statistical accounting practices are problematic, and thus, many are not taken seriously by police officers working the streets.

The following story, which illustrates this reason, is common and demonstrates the intrinsic flaws of statistical requirements:

A police substation in a large metropolitan area covered a considerable geographical area. The area of responsibility was eclectic and had a diverse population consisting of high, middle, and lower income communities. All of the officers assigned to this station had a minimum number of duty activities to perform monthly—felony arrest, traffic citations, and so on. Officers were assigned to specific areas at this substation and would work those areas consistently. An officer assigned to the lower income area had many felony arrests, but he failed to write the minimum number of traffic citations that were required. The officer's supervisor counseled him on his failure to meet the minimum citation standard and advised him that if he did not meet the standard for the next three months, his evaluation would reflect the deficiency in that performance. Although other officers working higher income areas met the standards set in all the performance categories, their felony arrests were half of the other officers working the lower income area. The officer working the lower income area requested to be reassigned to another area, where he would be able to meet the performance standards and thus avoid a negative performance rating. The officer was transferred to the other area. This transfer resulted in the officer meeting the statistical performance goals. But in the end, the overall goal of the department and the security of their community was compromised.

Police productivity measures are problematic. The goals of statistical practices are to hold police officers accountable, ensuring that the officers are using their time productively. The goal of statistics is to show tangible results. Sometimes the accountability method can be in conflict with the overall goal of the department. If officers believe that their department values flawed statistical programs over productivity, the goal of the department will suffer. But accountability and productivity is the wave of the future, and police officers will be expected to produce.

Reason Sixty-Eight: Accusations of sexual assault. No matter how careful an officer is, there will be a time or times when he will be accused of sexual assault after arresting a suspect. Being accused of sexual misconduct is just one of those situations that officers must be able to accept. Given that officers will be accused of such misconduct, officers need to be cognizant of what they say and how they act when conducting enforcement action involving suspects of the opposite sex. Although an officer could be accused of sexual misconduct with an individual of the same sex, this is rare and the odds are that it will not occur as compared to the former situation.

This story is typical for an officer who was accused of inappropriate contact with a suspect:

An officer made traffic stop and determined that the driver was intoxicated. After the officer informed the female driver that she would be arrested for driving while under the influence of alcohol, she began screaming and ripping her shirt off. The officer, at first, was in total shock, having never had a suspect react this way. He then attempted to place the suspect into handcuffs. By the time the officer was able to get the suspect into the patrol vehicle, she was naked from the waist up. The officer requested backup to assist in transporting the suspect to jail, but there were no other officers available. Two weeks later an internal investigation was started, because the complainant had accused the officer of sexual assault. Although the investigation resulted in an unsustained complaint, the officer was subjected to this kind of accusation. The officer stated that he always felt that others believed there was some thread of truth to the female's accusation, and that he felt tremendous embarrassment during the investigation. In the future, he would only contact women suspects when other officers were present.

Sexual allegations are examples of those things that officers must be aware of and do all that they can to avoid the appearance of sexual misconduct. But even if an officer has witnesses, this will not prevent sexual assault allegations. Therefore, just accept this as part of the job.

Reason Sixty-Nine: Threats. "I'll kill your family!" There is no doubt that this "I'll kill your family" threat is the most common threat that officers hear during their career. This threat has also caused numerous officers to lose their job or suffer disciplinary action, because they react emotionally to such a threat.

A story that demonstrates how a seasoned officer handles this threat is told in the following passage:

The officer, after arresting a known felony suspect, was transporting him to jail in his patrol vehicle. The suspect had put up a good fight prior to his arrest and had to be struck several times with the officer's baton. While being transported, the suspect started to say that he was going to "get" the officer if it was the last thing he ever did. The officer did not respond to the threats. The suspect, realizing that he wasn't getting a reaction from the officer, continued to say that he would "kill his mother." The officer responded that his mother had already passed away. The suspect then said he would kill his wife and children. The officer replied that he did not have a wife or children. The suspect became frustrated and asked, "Well, do you have a dog?" And the officer replied that he could kill the dog because the dog never listens to him anyway.

This story demonstrates one of the best ways to handle such idle threats. Some officers forget that suspects are trying to bait the officers into reacting emotionally. Suspects are aware of the chance of getting a charge reduced or possibly dismissed if they can bring charges against officers for police brutality.

Reason Seventy: Marriage—it's a hobby. Police officers marry, on average, three times throughout their careers. This has disastrous effects on an officer's financial, professional, and personal life. After retirement police officers receive a pension, and after each marriage that pension pie gets smaller and every bite gets a little more bitter.

This story comes from a 30-year veteran who has been married three times, and he relates the following:

I had planned to retire after just 25 years and have everything paid off, but unfortunately, those plans are gone as is a large percentage of my pension. I realize now that I will have to work until I die or they kick me out of here. I have no one to blame but myself and realize that having worked in this profession has taken its toll on my personal life. I don't believe that police work is conducive to married life because of the varied shift work and call-out that was required of me over the last 25 years.

The fact that officers will marry on average three times during their career is a factor that prospective police candidates should be aware of. Unlike other professions, officers transfer to other units or get promoted throughout their career, causing the officers to work a variety of shifts. The recurrent shift change is a major factor that results in considerable strain on married life.

Reason Seventy-One: "You can't please most of the people all of the time and you will never please all of the people all of the time." This reason demonstrates that most of the calls a police officer responds to will result in someone being dissatisfied with the police services rendered. As an officer comes to realize this quandary of never being able to satisfy everyone, he begins to hesitate when making a decision. Some officers start to base their decisions on whichever decision will cause them the least amount of resistance. Nevertheless, even this tactic does not always work.

This story demonstrates how an officer will never please all parties involved during a call and that any effort he makes to placate individuals is futile:

The officer, while responding and consequently investigating a minor traffic accident, knew that each driver was upset with the other and that each believed that the other was at fault. The officer realized that there was a possibility that one or both of the drivers might make a complaint on him. Therefore, the officer was overly attentive to the needs of the parties involved. The officer explained the report and actions both drivers should take to resolve the accident. After the incident, the officer believed that he had covered every possible aspect of the incident and thereby left both parties with nothing to complain about. Two days later, the officer was called into the supervisor's office and was advised that both parties made a complaint on him, each independent of the other. The complaints stated that both parties felt he spent a disproportionate amount of time with the other party.

Over time, police officers come to realize that they are in a no-win situation most of the time when responding to calls involving opposing interests. Situations that are win-win are rare because win-win situations don't usually involve police officer presence. The majority of decisions that police officers make can motivate a citizen to file a complaint, and that is a fact of policing that officers must learn to accept.

Reason Seventy-Two: Identifying yourself off duty. Officers come to realize that identifying themselves as police officers when off duty is a big mistake and the fewer people who know the better. There are two major reasons for police officers not to identify themselves off duty. First, as soon as a police officer identifies himself, all his actions from that instant forward will fall under department policies, and second, the officer's actions are subject to federal laws and guidelines. The federal law is usually referred to as the "Color of Law." The Color of Law federal statute generally states that any action or actions conducted by a police officer, after he identifies himself either visually or verbally, he will be held to all standards set forth by federal laws, on or off duty.

This story demonstrates the potential problem an officer encounters when he identifies himself off duty as a police officer:

The off-duty officer was walking in the downtown area, an area where the officer works. The officer was approached by a street salesman. The salesman asked the officer if he wanted to purchase any diamond jewelry for his wife or girlfriend, and the officer responded to the salesman with an emphatic "no." The salesman would not take no for an answer and became aggressive. As the salesman continued to walk alongside the officer, he continued his aggressive sales tactics. Then the salesman walked in front of the officer, obstructing his path and forcing the officer to walk around. Becom-

ing frustrated, the officer used colorful language, explaining that he was a cop and wanted to be left alone. When the officer held out his arm to push by the salesman off and to the side, the salesman dropped his merchandise. The salesman began to follow the police officer and started to yell that the officer had assaulted him and broke his merchandise. During this time, continuing to follow the off-duty officer, the salesman called the police department on his cell phone and told them he had been accosted by an officer and wanted the police to respond. The off-duty officer could hear the salesman on the phone and stopped to wait for the responding police. The result: the officer was found in violation of his department policy regarding conduct, using profanity when identifying himself as a police officer.

The above story relates how off-duty officers will be held to the same standards as when they are working. Although the above officer only identified himself to avoid further contact with the salesman, the officer miscalculated the salesman's response. This miscalculation is common, and seasoned officers realize that when they identify themselves off duty it usually results in making a situation worse.

Reason Seventy-Three: Your heart whispers, but the law speaks.
There will be several times throughout an officer's career when he must act according to the letter of the law. Although discretion is a major component of policing, there are situations that require an officer to act according to the law when their conscience dictates otherwise. Police work requires officers to make decisions and many of these decisions are discretionary. A police officer's discretion allows an officer to weigh all the circumstances, thus allowing the officer flexibility. Nevertheless, over the past several years, police departments and state laws have limited police officer discretion, mandating an officer to act in a specific

manner that can be contrary to how the officer would have acted if given discretionary power.

The following story demonstrates the dichotomy:

Officers responded to a domestic call. After arriving, the officers contacted a male who had custody of two children. The male's ex-wife was also at the residence and wanted to take the children to her home. The officer interviewed the couple, when the ex-wife stated that the male had struck her. The female had several red marks on her neck and appeared to have been physically battered. The male had several bruises on his arms and scratches on his face. The male told the officers that he had not touched his ex-wife. He also stated that his ex-wife's injuries had been self-inflicted prior to the arrival of the police officers. The male also stated that he realized that the law stated that one of the two had to go to jail and he did not want his children to see their mother going to jail; therefore, he would admit to striking her. Although the officer's intuition and gut feeling told them the male was speaking the truth, they had no choice and arrested the male for domestic violence.

This is an example that demonstrates a situation that limits officer discretion. There will be many situations that require an officer to act according to the letter of the law. Officers who fail to follow mandated guidelines or state laws requiring police officers to act are risking their careers. These types of situations that limit an officers ability to act in accordance with their conscience can cause officers to become apathetic and detached from family and friends.

Reason Seventy-Four: "Did that hamburger taste funny?" Someone messing with a cop's food? No, no, they wouldn't dare! Or would they? The fact is that somebody, sometime, somewhere will spit, throw on the floor, or do whatever can be imagined, to the platter of food a police officer ordered. Cooks, waiters, and bus persons will mess with a cop's food. This crime doesn't just occur at the local diner. The take-out order window, where the officer gulped down that burger while rushing off to the robbery call, might have a little something extra, at no extra charge.

This story tells of the worst-case scenario:

The officer, while working patrol on one of those nights when he would be lucky just to get a pee break, stopped off at the local drive-through to grab a burger and large drink, before heading of to the next emergency call. After he handled the call, he noticed that his stomach was upset and he began feeling a little queasy. He took another sip of the large soda and a bitter taste was noticed—one that he just now realized was there. The officer took off the lid to the soda and notice used toilet paper stuck to the bottom edge of the cup. The officer turned white and called the supervisor, who then called the paramedics. The establishment was shut down and the employee was arrested.

The fact is that unless an officer brown-bags his lunch, he will always be susceptible to the spiteful culinary employee. Officers will always wonder, after lunch, if the upset stomach is due to last night's meat loaf or the suspicious looking waiter who had a strange smile after serving the daily special.

Reason Seventy-Five: "Can you discipline my kid?" Citizens will expect police officers to solve their domestic family problems. Many problems that officers confront will not pertain to law enforcement. Conflicts between parents and children make up many disturbance calls that officers respond to, usually stemming from the child's failure to obey the parents' demands. The parents expect officers to correct the child's behavior with idle threats like "You will go to jail if you don't listen." Consequently, officer must act as social workers and attempt to give guidance to frustrated parents who have lost their children's respect.

This story tells a typical example of the diverse roles that officers are required and expected to perform for parents, with regard to their disruptive children:

The officer responded to a disturbance call that described a juvenile as being out of control. The parents told the arriving officers that their 13-year-old child would not listen to them and would not follow the rules of the house. The parents wanted the officer to tell their child to listen and obey their instructions or that he would take the child to jail. The officer, realizing how frustrated the parents were, agreed to make an attempt to communicate with their child. The child told the officer that he knew the officer couldn't do anything and that the officer should mind his own business. The officer turned to the parents and said, "I tried."

Officers are expected to wear a variety of hats. Citizens will expect officers to perform a variety of duties. Many of these duties will not have any remote relationship to law enforcement, but officers are expected to draw from their experience and use their perceived authoritative influence in a variety of situations.

Reason Seventy-Six: Giving up your rights. Every citizen is afforded certain inalienable rights by the Constitution of the United States. Most individuals who enter police work don't realize that some of these inalienable rights are forfeited. Officers' rights are usually limited by police department policies and regulations. Police organizations have the right to make restrictions on where officers live or limit the types of work officers pursue during their days off. In addition, police organizations have the right to discipline and terminate officers for violating policies that are contrary to state laws.

The story recounted here is based on a situation involving an officer who was being counseled by a supervisor:

The officer had what many administrators call a "personality conflict" with his supervisor. The officer had many counseling sessions with a particular supervisor, as did many of the officers on his squad. The supervisor had a reputation for using profanity and becoming verbally abusive and emotional during counseling sessions with officers. Most of the administration and officers in the department knew that the supervisor had emotional problems, but the administration failed to act in correcting the supervisor's conduct. The officer decided to take the situation into his own hands and surreptitiously tape his next counseling session with the supervisor. And as the officer predicted, the supervisor was abusive and violated the department policy regarding being professional and treating fellow officers with mutual respect. The officer took the taped session to the upper administration. The officer's action of taping his supervisor's misconduct resulted in a new department policy stating that officers will never covertly tape a fellow employee without the acknowledgment of both parties, although the state law under which the officer worked allowed one party consent taping.

Although the state law clearly stated that an individual can tape a conversation between two people without the knowledge of the other person and then replay that conversation to another person, police organizations can implement a policy that is more restrictive than court precedent. This more restrictive policy must be followed by officers or the officer may be subjected to an internal investigation. This reason is just one example of how a police department can implement policies that limit an officer's rights based only on the fact that he is a member of a police organization.

Reason Seventy-Seven: Financial woes—the least of your problems.
A candidate's finances are a factor police departments look at when hiring. After officers are hired, all their activities, finances, and leisure time can be subjected to scrutiny by the police department for which he works. Most of the larger departments have policies and standards that officers must adhere to with regard to conducting their finances. Some police departments require officers to get approval prior to filing for bankruptcy.

The following is a story told by an officer who found himself in financial distress:

The officer, after having suffered a failed marriage, let his spending exceed his paycheck. The officer started writing checks that his account could not cover. Then the officer would pay off one credit card with another. A major department store became a victim of the officer's bounced checks, and the department store manager knew that he was a police officer and contacted his department. Once they were contacted, they internally charged the officer with violating department policies. The internal investigation found the officer sustained on charges of failing to conduct his financial affairs in a responsible manner, bringing discredit to the police department.

Again, unlike work performed for the private sector, police departments hold officers to a higher standard. These higher standards apply to all aspects of life, personal and financial. If the police department wishes to implement policies relating to an officer's off-duty personal or financial activities, the officer will be expected to adhere to these higher standards.

Reason Seventy-Eight: Your health issues are the department's issues. As mentioned in the previous reason, an officer's health is also of interest to the police department, and confidentiality is not an option. Usually officers are required to submit to an annual physical. The results of the physical will be sent to an administrative detail staffed with civilian employees. Usually, after an annual physical, an officer will most likely receive some type of "corrective action" relating to the results of the physical. This corrective action can be any number of requests, such as that the employee needs to lose weight, reduce blood pressure, and so on, so the police department is indemnified if the officer fails to take the corrective action recommended.

The story that goes with this issue demonstrates how the annual physical has become a tactic to reduce police department liability at the expense of officers:

An officer went to his annual physical as he had done for the past fifteen years. The officer was an avid runner, running at least three miles every day. His annual physical results stated "corrective action" due to the officer's blood test showing that his good cholesterol was low. The action recommended the officer increase his exercise or risk forfeiting health benefits. After receiving the notice, the officer called the civilian person responsible for noting corrective actions and asked just how many more miles did he need to run in a day, since his minimum of three miles was obviously not sufficient. The officer did not receive any further advice from the civilian staff.

One of the benefits of working as a police officer is the annual physical. But the drawback is that officers' health information will not be confidential. Police departments constantly look for ways to indemnify themselves from liability. Sometimes this indemnification comes at the expense of officers. And like most large government programs, no matter how good the program's intentions are, the organization attempts to duck responsibility when the checks are due.

Reason Seventy-Nine: Aversion to the terminally ill is not an option. Police officers will come into contact with every possible disease that society has to offer, and many of these diseases are extremely contagious. Unfortunately there will be times when officers will contract illnesses from people because of the close physical contact required in various law enforcement activities. These include experiences with combative subjects who will have open wounds from which the officer may be exposed to bodily fluids, or having an arrested subject in the patrol vehicle, where the close proximity and ventilation create a situation for the officer to become exposed to an infectious illness.

The following story is from an officer who contracted an infectious illness:

The officer served several years in the police department as a patrol officer working some of the worst areas in the city. The officer knew that many subjects he had arrested had infectious diseases. The officer had knowledge of the health risks involved when dealing with high risk individuals such as drug users and prostitutes, and therefore he took all the possible precautions like wearing protective gloves and washing his hands as often as possible. After the officer's annual physical, the civilian staff notified him that he had contracted a form of hepatitis.

Officers will be expected to confront individuals and physically take them into custody. Some of them will have contagious illnesses, thereby exposing an officer to their illness. Each year, several officers contract illnesses that affect their life and, consequently, affect the lives of their friends and family.

Reason Eighty: A cop is a cop is a cop. Police officers are suspicious people by nature, and if they aren't, they will be after just a few years of service. The five W's—What, When, Where, Why, and Who—are programmed into the psyches of officers. Once this programming is set into the mental processes of an officer, he will automatically interact with other people in a Q and A format to find out what the five W's are. This Q and A format gives individuals a feeling of being interrogated, especially if they have not interacted with police in the past.

The following story tells of an incident with an officer and his wife while they were out having dinner with another couple:

The off-duty officer and his wife were out having dinner with one of his wife's coworkers and the coworker's spouse. During dinner, the off-duty officer, never having met the other couple, began to ask the couple questions, one after the other. The officer was automatically covering the five W's, when the wife noticed the couple becoming uncomfortable with the rapid questioning. The wife politely told the other couple that they would have to forgive her husband for the inquisition, saying, "Now you know what it is like living with a cop—a cop is a cop is a cop," and they all laughed and the dinner was a success.

Police are inquisitive people and after a number of years, this inquisitiveness, which is required if an officer is to be successful, will become a part of his personality. Police work is a career that affects and changes an individual's behavior and personality. Family and friends must understand that an officer's personality and behaviors will change, and understanding these changes will help to preserve personal relationships.

Reason Eighty-One: Learn to act. An important skill that officers must develop is acting. Although there will be many situations in which an officer must control his emotions when interacting with suspects, there are just as many times when an officer must act as if he cares about another individual's problems, even when that individual has created the problem.

The following story involves an officer who failed to use this skill and the embarrassment he suffered:

An officer responded to a disturbance call involving a male subject who had walked through an apartment complex creating a disturbance. The officer arrived at the apartment complex and discovered a trail of blood that led from a broken window, through the apartment complex, to the subject's apartment. The paramedics had already arrived and were inside apartment as the officer entered. The officer observed the two paramedics treating the subject on the floor of the apartment, but was not able to view the subject or his injuries. The officer expected the subject to have minor injuries because of the broken window. After one of the paramedics stood up and faced the officer, the officer saw that the subject had suffered a gash to his right arm that exposed all the bone and muscle from the shoulder to the wrist. The officer, not expecting to see such a serious injury, yelled, "Oh my God!" The subject had been calm, but after he heard the reaction of the officer to his injury, he started to yell, "Am I going to die?" The officer realized that he had caused the subject to become agitated, and then the paramedics had to deal with calming the subject to stabilize him for transportation to the hos-

pital. The officer was embarrassed and turned and walked out of the apartment. To this day, the paramedic hasn't forgiven the officer.

Officers need to learn to act because their reactions can influence a situation. The actions of others and the situations they interject themselves into will no doubt shock and amaze officers. Prepare for the unexpected and learn to act accordingly.

Reason Eighty-Two: "Report for duty? But it's Christmas..." Police officers work during every holiday, 24 hours a day, 365 days a year. Police are required to work and will be called for duty at the most inconvenient times. If this requirement is contradictory to one's beliefs or family values, then that individual should reconsider a career in law enforcement.

The following story is related by a three-year veteran who was working for a large department. The story is a typical example of what is required by police officers:

The three-year officer was working on a senior squad, and for the first time in three years, he was going to get Christmas Day off. The officer requested the day off two months ahead of time and it seemed like everything was in order. For the first Christmas in three years, he would be spending the day with his family. During Christmas Eve, another officer became injured and the supervisor told the officer that due to minimum staffing levels, he would be required to work.

Whether an officer works patrol or a specialized unit, working holidays is just one of the things they are expected to do. Officers will be required to work during those times that many believe are for family and friends. Police candidates often fail to consider the obligations that will be required from a career in law enforcement.

Reason Eighty-Three: "Who's that in the rearview mirror?" Police officers develop what officers call a healthy paranoia. This paranoia manifests in several ways, for example, officers will almost always sit facing the entrance of a restaurant or waiting area after entering a building, with his/her back against a wall, scanning the room for potential threats. These seemingly unnatural behaviors for the average citizen become second nature to a police officer after years of service. Whether a police officer is on or off duty, he views the world from a law enforcement perspective.

The following story demonstrates this healthy paranoia and is told by an officer who was shocked by the reaction of his new girlfriend:

The officer had been working as a policeman for several years and was married, but like many police officers, found that marriage is a difficult partnership to maintain. After his divorce, he began dating and started a new relationship. He felt his new girlfriend had understood of the hours he worked and appeared to adjust well to his sometimes controlling nature. After a night out, they were driving to his home. On the way to his house, he thought a vehicle was following them, and without a word to his girlfriend, drove past his residential turnoff. The girlfriend inquired why he was passing his street. He said he thought that they might have been followed and did not want to risk turning into his driveway and divulging the location of his home. He realized at that point that his girlfriend did not fully understand what he did for a living or the type of individuals that he had contact with on a daily basis. He explained to her that he was just more aware of potential threats than the average person, "just a healthy paranoia that's all." The girlfriend told him that she did not want to develop a healthy paranoia, and they went their separate ways.

The fact is that police officers have a more heightened sense of awareness about their surroundings than the average citizen. Some friends and wives can understand and accept the heightened awareness officers develop and realize it is a part of the officer's job that cannot simply be turned off and on. Although an officer's suspicious nature is a naturally occurring sense of self-preservation, it can create barriers when forming relationships.

Reason Eighty-Four: Freedom of speech—mum's the word. The U.S. Supreme Court has indicated that "the state has interests as an employer in regulation of the speech of its employees (police officers) that differ significantly from those it possesses in connection with regulation of the speech of the citizenry in general." The restrictions depend on several factors, including the impact of the statements, the truthfulness, the manner of how the statements are relayed, and the position of the officer making the statements.

The following story tells of an officer who wanted to bring to light a problem he had encountered during a dispute between the police administration and the police union:

The officer spent several thousand dollars in attorney fees and hours of his own time to bring about a change regarding police administrative policies—policies that the police union would not address. During the court proceedings, there were many facts that came to light regarding misfeasance and malfeasance, but the court ruled that the officer filing the case would be censured to all and any of the court findings, because the employer, the police department, has the right to censor officers and restrict their right of free speech if that speech undermines the authority of the administrative staff.

As mentioned in some of the other reasons, police officers do not have the same rights and privileges that citizens have. Higher ranking officers have more restrictions placed on their speech than line officers. As a general policy implemented by police departments, officers who talk to reporters without the permission of a supervisor can receive disciplinary action. This restriction of speech has been established by years of court precedent and needs to be considered when choosing law enforcement as a career.

Reason Eighty-Five: No recourse: "But he lied." Most officers who have worked with an internal investigative unit will tell you that a large percentage of complaints filed by citizens against a police officer are embellished or outright lies. Nevertheless, police departments spend thousands of dollars each year investigating these fictitious complaints. The officers who have these fallacious complaints filed on them will have absolutely no recourse against the complainant.

The following story demonstrates what every officer will have to confront; most will have to deal with these internal investigations several times throughout their career:

The officer was notified that he was the subject of an internal investigation alleging that he took a bribe to write a citation to a citizen as the result of a traffic accident. During the investigation, the officer told the investigator that he had a witness to the incident and that he recorded the total interaction with the complainant. The tape was given to the investigator and the officer was cleared of any wrongdoing after a lengthy interview process. The officer filed a libel lawsuit against the citizen, but the state court had ruled that a police officer cannot file a suit against a citizen even if it is found that the citizen's complaint was found to be fictitious and baseless.

Many state courts prohibit officers from filing lawsuits against citizens who file fictitious complaints. What most prospective police candidates do not realize is that these fictitious complaints take a toll on officer moral. Police officers have a strong sense of fairness, and when an internal investigation, prompted by slanderous, baseless allegations, results in an unfounded disposition, there will be no apologies to the officer. Officers will face several baseless internal investigations. Although officers are held accountable for every word they speak, they will come to realize that complainants will not be held accountable for any lies, written or spoken. Even the most resilient officer will become affected by the slanderous allegations that continually subject him to internal investigations. This results in officers becoming bitter and negative about their career.

Reason Eighty-Six: Can't eat there anymore. Police officers come into contact with and arrest all types of people. As stated in the discussion for reason seventy-four, officers must be mindful of the ramifications of the person they arrest. A situation that affects all officers working in a specific area is when the arrestee is the resident cook at the favorite eating spot. This arrest has a great impact on the officers who work the grave-yard shift, because there are limited restaurants open during the night. But it always seems to happen—the local cook working during the grave-yard shift gets arrested for one thing or another.

The following story is one that almost every officer can relate too:

After a long, hard shift, officers arrived at debriefing. The officers start filing into the briefing room, completing the shift reports, and joking about the shift's events. The last officer arrived and walked right up to the briefing board and wrote the following: "Don't eat at Joe's Diner." The officer then turned and told his squad that he had just arrested Joe for DUI. The officers responded with a big sigh, as one of the officers said, "That was the best eat spot."

The fact of police work is that some of the people who officers interact with throughout their daily routine will become victims or suspects. Sometimes the arrest of a person will affect places that officers patronize. When these subjects come in contact with the police, whether victims or arrestees, the officer's responsibility is to inform other officers of these events.

Reason Eighty-Seven: "What's that smell?" Police are called to situations in which people are highly emotional and intoxicated, and thus, officers will witness people in situations when they are at their worst. Many of these situations will include people having lost all bodily functions. Even when individuals have "accidents," officers are still required to take physical control of, search, and make arrests of these subjects. An officer must have a strong stomach and be able to breathe out of his mouth for long periods of time.

The following story illustrates contacting people at their worst:

An officer working patrol pulls up next to a motorist at a red light. As the officer looked to his right, he noticed that the driver had a familiar expression on his face. The officer recognized this facial expression as an expression he had seen many times in the past. The officer knew the driver was DUI, and his suspicion was confirmed when he glanced downward and saw that the entire driver's door was covered with barf. After pulling the driver over, the officer started to approach the vehicle when he noticed a familiar mixture of smells. The officer thought, "I'll never get that smell out of my patrol vehicle." The driver failed the sobriety test and was off to jail.

Officers are expected to handle people at their worst. There is no way an officer can avoid situations in which people have defecated, vomited, or urinated on themselves. A common saying in police work is "You catch him, you clean him." Police officers are required to handle these situations with professionalism and grace.

Reason Eighty-Eight: As long as you do your job and keep your nose clean, you'll have nothing to worry about. The law enforcement profession is no different than any other profession with regard to climbing the corporate ladder—luck, timing, and playing the political game will determine an officer's success. The political game in the police field can be summed up in this way: who the officer knows and the contacts he makes within the department will determine if he achieves his goals. As a general rule, even if an officer continually exceeds performance standards, his performance will not carry much weight when applying for a specialized unit.

The following story demonstrates the human factor within a police agency and how the "personality conflict" dictates administrative action:

An officer demonstrated his abilities by consistently producing the highest statistics on the squad. The officer was motivated and wanted to develop a reputation as a hard charger. He hoped to test for the police SWAT team. The officer had all the training he needed to be successful when testing for the unit. But unfortunately, a personality conflict came into play when the officer started to interject opinions that his supervisor was opposed to. The officer never imagined that his supervisor would attempt to block his goal for testing for the SWAT unit, until another supervisor came to him and told him that he should transfer to another squad away from his present supervisor or he would never make the SWAT team. The officer believed that if he continued to work hard, nothing his supervisor could do would stop him. The officer never achieved his goal and, reflecting back, realized that doing your job and keeping your nose clean does not always result in accomplishing your goal in a police organization.

Police organizations usually don't consider productivity a criterion for selecting officers for specialized units. An officer's productivity can be subjectively measured by his supervisor, and a personality conflict will affect an officer's career goals. The system breeds cronyism, favoritism, and nepotism, and if an officer does not fit the mold and play the political game, he is not likely to accomplish his career goals.

Reason Eighty-Nine: "Yes, I know it was an honest mistake—sign here!" Internal police investigations usually occur on two levels. The first level is when an officer is charged with a minor infraction of a department policy, in which case it is usually handled by the officer's supervisor. The second level of investigation is of a more serious nature and involves internal affairs investigators. In either case, the investigative process is stressful. In addition, internal investigations can also be categorized into two types. The first type involves police officers who have made a mistake in judgment that can be interpreted by an investigator as a policy violation, and the second type involves the actions of an officer when the officer knows his actions are in violation of department policy. Sometimes these two categories are referred to as "a mistake of the heart (not an intentional act to violate policy) or a mistake of the mind (knowingly violating policy)." Mistakes of the mind are not as difficult for officers to face up to, and although no one likes to admit he has made a mistake, most officers will accept the discipline as long as it is fair. The problem that occurs in police departments today is when an officer's actions result in an interpretation of a policy violation that occurred when the officer was performing his duties, and there was no intention to violate any rule or regulation.

The following story illustrates an officer's mistake in judgment:

An officer who had just over six months on the job was motivated and knew that he had found his niche in life. After making an arrest, the officer completed the necessary paperwork, booking the suspect into the city jail. After the subject was booked, a correction officer discovered a miniature pocket knife in a small front pocket of the suspect's pants. The arresting officer's supervisor was informed of the incident and conducted an investigation, charging the arresting officer with neglect of duty, with regard to failing to discover the pocket knife during the initial search of the suspect. Although, the officer stated that he searched the suspect and followed department policy the fact that he had missed the knife on the search was the issue. The officer's supervisor found the officer guilty of the charge and gave the officer discipline, resulting in a negative performance review that went into his personal file for an extended period of time.

Police officers will make mistakes, and whether or not the mistake is considered understandable will have little weight in the internal investigation. Monday morning quarterbacking is the rule. Officers are expected to follow policies, rules, and regulations. Officers who make honest mistakes will still be held accountable, and the more productive an officer is, the greater chance he will be disciplined for an honest mistake.

Reason Ninety: You carry a gun and have the power to take away someone's freedom but are treated like a child. Police organizations are notorious for writing knee-jerk policies based on the poor judgment of one officer, as opposed to dealing directly with an officer and his irresponsible behavior. Police administrators generalize a specific officer's irresponsible action and attempt to write policy that addresses the action. Knee-jerk reactions by police administrators are viewed by officers as failures in leadership. Generalizations by administrators create animosity with line officers who have handled their duties with maturity and professionalism.

The following story gives an example of a police administrator who did generalize the actions of one officer, thus restricting the actions of all officers:

An officer was spending every minute of his downtime at a local coffee shop. The manager of the coffee shop wrote a letter complaining about the amount of time the officer spent at his shop. The manager stated that his employees were not able to concentrate on their duties because the officer continually talked to employees during their shifts. After the police administration read the coffee shop manager's letter, a new department policy was written prohibiting all officers from patronizing the coffee shop.

Police administrations tend to generalize problems instead of dealing with a specific behavioral issue of an individual. Officers view this administrative action as punishing the whole because of the actions of one officer, and they interpret these administrative responses as treating them like children.

Reason Ninety-One: The supervisor who doesn't care. Police officers categorize supervisors into three types. The first is the supervisor who is motivational and is a leader, the second is the supervisor who doesn't care, and the third is the supervisor who believes it is his or her job to get rid of an officer. The latter supervisor will be discussed in the next reason. The first supervisor is the one everyone wants to work for because there is no problem for officers or the administration. The supervisor who doesn't care is one who doesn't want an officer to do anything innovative or proactive. The supervisor who doesn't care doesn't want any problems and he requires that officers do just enough to meet the minimum standards.

This story was told by a senior officer who worked for this kind of supervisor:

The officer wanted to address a homeless problem in his area of responsibility. The homeless people were generating several calls for service, and the local businesses wanted the officer's assistance and advice in dealing with the problem. The officer wrote up a plan that incorporated several other units to assist in addressing the problem. After approaching his supervisor with the plan, his supervisor told him that he should just handle his calls for service and not generate new projects that would more than likely cause the homeless advocates to generate complaints against him and the department.

Police supervisors set the tone for officers. If the supervisor is motivated and creative, he will inspire officers to be innovative. Motivated supervisors who have leadership abilities are few in number. Supervisors who don't care and require the minimum performance standard will not assist officers in achieving their career goals. Unfortunately, most officers will encounter the uncaring, unmotivated supervisor more then once throughout their career.

Reason Ninety-Two: The supervisor who wants to get rid of you. This type of supervisor can create a great deal of stress and burnout for officers. Although this supervisor's motivations to go after an officer are personal, the supervisor believes that the administration has anointed him with knowing who should or who should not be a part of the organization. These supervisors are usually classified as "paper tigers" and will hang paper (discipline) on an officer for any and everything. This paper tiger will target one or two officers on a squad, documenting every mistake they make in an attempt to make an example to other officers. What most officers don't understand is that these supervisors don't view their actions as personal vendettas—they see themselves as being anointed by the police administration. Thus if the supervisor has a personality conflict with an officer, it is his job to document the officer's actions and bring the officer into line with the administration, because if the supervisor doesn't like the officer, neither would the police administration.

The following story demonstrates this type of supervisor:

The supervisor had a personality conflict with one of his officers. The officer was called into the supervisor's officer on a weakly basis and asked to explain whatever action the officer had taken regarding a specific incident. The officer knew the supervisor was documenting all his calls and was usually prepared for the weekly meeting. Every time the officer was called into the supervisor's office, he had his statistics call-sheet in hand, showing that he was one of the top performers on the squad. The supervisor always admitted that the officer's performance was not the issue. The officer would then ask what the supervisor's problem was. The supervisor stated that he thought that he was a disruptive element to the team spirit, but never was able to articulate how he was disruptive. The interesting twist to this story is that the supervisor was eventually terminated and the officer became a supervisor for the department.

Officers, at one time or another, will work for a paper tiger. These supervisors usually target specific officers, officers they feel threatened by. These supervisors actions create stress for all officers, because others know they could be the next example.

Reason Ninety-Three: De-policing: De-policing is a phenomenon that has developed over the last ten years. The phenomenon has also been referred to as tactical disengagement or detachment. The result of de-policing is a reduction in proactive policing. De-policing can be defined as: a measurable reduction in productivity compared to the "normal" standard of an organization, and the cause of the reduction in productivity is a conscious or unconscious belief that performing one's duties will result in greater risk to negative sanctions, that is, citizen complaints resulting in an internal investigation, public scrutiny, and/ or when individuals or organizations fail to act on criminal trends and conduct investigations due to the beliefs that negative sanctions and/or negative public response will result from performing their organiza- tion's mission.

De-policing can occur at all levels of a police organization from patrol officers and supervisors to police administrations, but the focus here is how it affects the line officers.

The adage that one hears from line officers relating to de-policing is: "More work, more problems—no work, no problems." And the story that is common in policing resulting from de-policing is as follows:

An officer just returned from his second internal investigation, and both investigations had involved charging the officer with discourtesy toward a citizen. After the last investigation, the officer approached his supervisor and requested a desk position that would limit contact with the public. The supervisor asked why the officer wanted to transfer to such a boring post. The officer explained that, although the complaints against him were found to be false, he was not able to perform proactively because he was fearful that he would be subjected to another internal investigation. The officer confessed, "The risk is too great, and I want to test for a specialized assignment without the risk of being disciplined."

De-policing has become a huge problem in police departments, and police administrators are not willing to discuss the topic. Police administrators are fearful that if de-policing is recognized as a problem in their departments, they will be the ones held responsible to develop solutions. Most administrators will only admit behind closed doors that de-policing is occurring, but the administrative public message is: "There is no evidence pointing to de-policing being a problem in this agency." Usually there is evidence that points to de-policing and it can be measured in a number of ways, including reduced citizen contacts and reduced arrest rates. Officers realize that the more proactive they are, the more likely they will be subjected to an internal complaint. If the police department's complaint process does not take officers' concerns into consideration, de-policing will continually be a productivity problem in the future.

Reason Ninety-Four: Stereotyped. Most professionals that serve the community, such as teachers, firemen, or pilots, have only positive stereotypes. Policing, on the other hand, is one of the few public-service professions that has just as many negative as positive stereotypes.

The story that demonstrates these negative stereotypes was told by an officer who had just begun to realize these negative images people have of police officers:

The officer's child requested that he speak to the class during "Professional Day" at the child's grammar school. But two days later, the child asked his father not to come to the event. After the father asked why, the child stated that other children in the school told him that police shoot and hit people for no reason. The father asked his child if he believed what the other children had said. The child responded "no," but still did not want his dad to speak at the school.

Police officers represent authority. Authority figures have always been viewed as a necessary evil in modern society. Police exemplify the authority figure, and some children as well as adults view police as a repressive symbol of society. The negative stereotypes that many people have of police will never change, and officers must understand that no matter how well citizens are treated, the police will always be viewed as acolytes of the wealthy to oppress the poor. Officers will find that any attempt to change an individual's negative attitudes about the police is a waste of their time.

Reason Ninety-Five: Evaluating a threat—it's part of the job. Police officers learn many skills during their years of service. One of the most important skills officers learn is to evaluate a physical threat. The basic concept that officers learn is to watch the hands, because the hands are the part of the person that will have the knife, gun, or other dangerous object that can injure the officer. These observation skills do not turn off after an officer leaves the shift.

The following story illustrates evaluation of the threat:

An off-duty officer was out with his wife and children for dinner and a movie. The officer's wife noticed that every time her husband spoke to someone he would always scan the person up and down. The wife asked why he did this, and her husband replied that he was unaware of doing it. The wife responded, "I guess that's just a cop thing." Both of them laughed, but the officer never wanted to tell his wife the real reason—because he never wanted her to feel that she had to be on guard as he felt that he had to be.

Many new officers will have difficulty adjusting to a profession that requires them to be wary of others on and off duty. Evaluation of a threat is a necessary skill that will become programmed into the officer's behavior both on and off duty.

Reason Ninety-Six: The civilian factor. Over the last twenty years, police organizations hired civilian employees to perform supportive police functions. The hiring of civilian employees brings many benefits to a police organization. The problem police officers encounter with civil employees usually stems from situations in which an officer does not get the support that he expects from the civilian unit. After several incidents in which the officer does not receive the service he expects, he starts to feel that he is in a supporting role and the civilians are the focus of the organization's goals.

The story that illustrates the civilian factor is as follows:

An officer on patrol observed a suspicious vehicle and began to follow the driver. The officer called over his radio to the dispatcher to run the license plate for wants, that is, "stolen" or possibly a felony vehicle. The dispatcher did not respond to the officer's first radio request, and he had to ask the dispatcher a second time, saying, "Control, did you copy my request?" The officer knew that this dispatcher was extremely moody and would take offense if the she thought that the officers in the field were not being polite in their radio requests. Officers complained in the past about the dispatcher's unprofessional demeanor, but the dispatcher would complain about officers who complained about her. The stalemate resulted with the officer being counseled for insensitivity.

The civilian factor is just another example of when officers must understand that they and they only will be held to a higher standard of conduct. Civilians perform all types of duties in police organizations, from dispatchers to criminal technicians. The interface between police and civilians has always been a tenuous one. Officers will no doubt hear other officers ask, "Who works for who, around here?" As a result of the different standards for civilians, officers will become frustrated with the lack of professionalism required from civilians.

Reason Ninety-Seven: The Disgruntled Cop Syndrome. From years of being caught between the bureaucracy of police organizations and the negative nature of the job, police work can turn the most positive employee into a disgruntled, bitter, and negative person. A disgruntled cop can be easily identified after a minute of conversation. Police officers who become bitter and negative don't attempt to hide their feelings toward the police administration or supervision. Historically, the syndrome didn't manifest in an officer until he became a fifteen-or twenty-year veteran. But because of the contemporary demands of modern police work, the Disgruntled Cop Syndrome is occurring earlier in a police officer's career.

The following story is of a disgruntled police officer and how a typical administrator reacts to his negativity:

During a morning briefing the administrative sergeant of a station entered the briefing room. The sergeant wanted to receive feedback from the officers regarding a new department policy that was being drafted. After the sergeant spoke, he asked for the feedback from the officers. The disgruntled officer told the sergeant that he didn't like the proposed policy and continued to generalize about how it was an attempt by the police department to duck responsibility by placing more restrictions on officers. The sergeant became frustrated and told the officer, "If you can't say anything positive, don't say anything at all."

The story is a typical example of a disgruntled officer and how police administrators usually react to comments made by disgruntled employees. Police officers become disgruntled for several reasons. The main problem with a disgruntled police officer is that the behavior is contagious and will begin to affect other officers if it is not dealt with. Most police administrations do not effectively handle the disgruntled police officer, and therefore, the behavior spreads throughout the department.

Reason Ninety-Eight: Selective amnesia. Selective amnesia occurs when an officer asks a favor of another officer he knows, or knew. In such cases, the officer who asks the favor has forgotten a negative incident that occurred between them and has no idea of his own poor reputation for not doing anything for anyone unless it benefits himself.

The following story involves a retired supervisor who requests a favor from an officer, even though the retired supervisor had consistently given the officer a difficult time in the past when he was on patrol:

I was eating at the local diner when a retired supervisor approached me and asked me if I could do him a favor. He wanted me to tell other officers that he had started a consulting firm, hoping that I would spread the word of his business. I couldn't believe that he would ask any cop in this department for anything, because this retired supervisor would hang paper (discipline) on every cop he could for anything—his reputation in the department was mud.

Selective amnesia occurs quite frequently in police departments. An officer who has a reputation for being unfair or for not doing anything for anyone unless it benefits him, is exhibiting selective amnesia when he asks for favors from other officers whom he has mistreated in the past. Most of the time these officers or supervisors have no concept of how others perceive them, and they have no idea that their reputations are viewed by officers as unprofessional and selfish.

Reason Ninety-Nine: "Retired? Who Cares?" For any person, retiring is a huge life-changing event. Prior to retiring, a police officer has spent twenty-five years or more going to work, dressing in his uniform, and hitting the streets. Generally, police officers are individuals who have not diversified their lives. Police officers who are retiring have spent a lifetime chasing the bad guy. When the retired cop gets the opportunity to talk to other, younger cops, he will usually only receive short one-line answers.

The story that illustrates this reason is as follows:

A police officer who had been retired for several years was working for a security company and saw two patrol officers talking in his security area. The two cops where talking side-by-side in their patrol vehicles when the retired officer approached the officers and asked how they were doing. The retired officer wanted to engage the two younger officers in a conversation, telling them that he had been a cop for thirty years. The retired officer said that the two officers just looked at him as if he were bothering them. The retired officer realized that cops don't want to hear the phrase, "I was a cop once," nor did he when he was a cop.

Police officers relate to officers who are currently working as police. Officers who have retired are generally viewed as people who worked during a different time with different rules. Retired officers are not elevated to a higher status or viewed as individuals who can advise officers on police matters because police tactics and policies change rapidly. Retirement is extremely difficult for police officers who have always seen themselves as officers and not as civilians.

Reason One Hundred: Retirement is short lived. The number of years a police officer lives after retirement is far less than the average professional. Historically, the average number of years that police officers lived after retirement was five years. Of course, now police officers are living longer after retirement, but compared to the average retired person, police don't live nearly as long. Police studies have suggested several causal factors for police dying earlier than other professionals. Many of the studies have focused on the physiological and psychological stresses that are unique to police work. These studies can be easily researched on any Criminal Justice website.

The following story is typical, and unfortunately it will be the story that many police officers experience:

An officer was an avid runner, running over fifty miles a week. The officer had more than thirty years of experience and could retire any time that he wanted with 90 percent of his present pay. As a result, the officer was working for only 10 percent of his present pay, because if he didn't work, he would be getting a retirement check totaling 90 percent of what the department was paying him. The officer always said that he was going to retire within the year, but he never did. Then, one day he was working out at the local gym and suffered a massive heart attack. The officer will never enjoy the years of retirement owed to him for his dedication to the community.

The fact is that many officers will not retire until it is too late or until their health and quality of life have diminished. Officers don't realize the toll that the career has taken on their health until they become stricken with an illness forcing them into retirement. Choosing a career as a police officer will most likely take years off a person's life.

Reason One Hundred One: Ninety percent of the job is negative. Prospective police candidates should ask themselves if the last one hundred reasons are worth enduring time and time again throughout a twenty-five-to thirty-year career. This last reason is the one reason that a person should contemplate for a long time before committing to a career in law enforcement. Although there will be positive events, the majority of experiences that officers witness are negative. Officers continually contact people who have been victims, and officers will not be able to help them recover from their traumatic events.

The story told here is a simple one, but the story tells it like it is:

An officer was at a local restaurant and overheard a conversation between a couple talking about how police are corrupt. The officer heard one of the individuals say the following: "Have you ever noticed that police are always around when something bad has happened? Why is that—doesn't that make you suspicious?" After that comment, it took all the officer could do to hold his tongue, but the officer knew that addressing the couple would not change their opinion of police.

Police officers are a necessary element of a society. The majority of police work is reacting to calls when something "bad" has occurred. Although a citizen may have a problem that requires a police response, the citizen is in a situation that he does not want to be in, and he wishes that whatever had happened hadn't. The police officer is a part of that negative experience, thus people will consciously and unconsciously identify police with their traumatic event.

Conclusion: So, you still want to be a cop?

As I have stated, the motivation for writing this book is to inform the prospective police candidate about the negatives of a career in law enforcement. I want the candidate to enter police work with a thorough understanding of what to expect. I have seen too many young men and women enter the field and become disillusioned and bitter. In an effort to hire as many qualified applicants as possible, many police administrations have failed to be forthright with the challenges of such a demanding career. It is a career that takes its toll on a person's physiological and psychological health, and only after having spent thousands of taxpayer dollars do police organizations make attempts at counseling police officers' families regarding the candidates' behavioral changes.

Police organizations should acknowledge the benefits of ensuring that candidates are well informed before recruiting them into an academy. Having candidates who are informed before entering the field will result in fewer resignations and fewer mediocre employees. Informed candidates will be mentally and physiologically prepared for the stresses, reducing the dropout rates during officers' first years of service, which then benefits the police department and the community, saving valuable training time and money. In addition, the risk of a police candidate becoming disillusioned with police work is reduced.

I've listed 101 reasons why you should not become a police officer. You may say, "Why not list 101 reasons *to* become a police officer—I could have easily listed 101 reason to become a police officer," But I will only state one reason and that is: If you want to be a part of a career that has internal personal rewards, to protect your community and to be a part of a philosophy that contributes to the progress of society, then choose law enforcement for your career. I did. Good luck in your decision.

978-0-595-35136-7
0-595-35136-0

9 780595 351367